201 ORGANIC BABY PURÉES

The Freshest, Most Wholesome Food Your Baby Can Eat!

TAMIKA L. GARDNER, founder of SimplyBabyFoodRecipes.net

AVON, MASSACHUSETTS

Published by
Adams Media, a division of F+W Media, Inc.
57 Littlefield Street, Avon, MA 02322. U.S.A.
www.adamsmedia.com

Contains material adapted and abridged from *The Everything® Organic Cooking for Baby and Toddler Book* by Kim Lutz and Megan Hart, MS, RD,
copyright © 2008, F+W Media, Inc., ISBN 10: 1-59869-926-1, ISBN 13: 978-1-59869-926-5; and *The Everything® Cooking for Baby and Toddler Book*
by Shana Priwer and Cynthia Phillips, with technical review by Vincent Iannelli, MD, copyright © 2006, F+W Media, Inc., ISBN 10: 1-59337-691-X,
ISBN 13: 978-1-59337-691-8.

ISBN-10: 1-4405-2899-3
ISBN-13: 978-1-4405-2899-6
eISBN-10: 1-4405-3051-3
eISBN-13: 978-1-4405-3051-7

Printed in the United States of America.

10   9   8   7   6

Library of Congress Cataloging-in-Publication Data
is available from the publisher.

This publication is designed to provide accurate and authoritative information with regard to the subject matter covered. It is sold with the understand-ing that the publisher is not engaged in rendering legal, accounting, or other professional advice. If legal advice or other expert assistance is required, the services of a competent professional person should be sought.
—From a *Declaration of Principles* jointly adopted by a Committee of the American Bar Association and a Committee of Publishers and Associations

This book is intended as general information only and should not be used to diagnose or treat any health condition. In light of the complex, individual, and specific nature of health problems, this book is not intended to replace professional medical advice. The ideas, procedures, and suggestions in this book are intended to supplement, not replace, the advice of a trained medical professional. Consult your physician before adopting any of the sugges-tions in this book, as well as about any condition that may require diagnosis or medical attention. The author and publisher disclaim any liability arising directly or indirectly from the use of this book.

Many of the designations used by manufacturers and sellers to distinguish their product are claimed as trademarks. Where those designations appear in this book and Adams Media was aware of a trademark claim, the designations have been printed with initial capital letters.

This book is available at quantity discounts for bulk purchases.
For information, please call 1-800-289-0963.

DEDICATION

This book is dedicated to my loving husband and amazing children
who inspire me every day—Troy, Nikai, and Troy II.

ACKNOWLEDGMENTS

I would like to express my sincere gratitude to all my family for continuing to push me to fulfill my dreams! Especially my mother, who, not knowing the reason, a couple of years ago had a premonition and told me to make recipes every day. This book is the outcome of that. Thank you mom. David, thank you for all your ideas that keep my mind on overdrive. Dad, thank you for giving me an entrepreneurial spirit and drive to be the best. To Dr. Colman and Dr. Schillings at the Pediatric Specialists of Bloomfield Hills, thank you for your guidance and providing excellent care for my children. To Dr. Joelle Mays and family, thank you for being so helpful and influential in more ways than you know. Special thanks to my mother-in-law and extended family for being so supportive. Helen, Layna, Aaran, and Deborah, you all had a profound impact in my life. Lastly, thank you, Victoria Sandbrook, for presenting this opportunity and Wendy Simard for your guidance and hard work on this book.

CONTENTS

CHAPTER 5: More Flavor to Savor (Eight or Nine Months): Introducing Semismooth Purées...78

CHAPTER 6: Pleasing an Expanded Palate (Ten to Twelve Months): Chunky Purées for Little Ones...135

CHAPTER 7: **Fun and Fingerlicious Food (Twelve Months and Beyond): Transitional Meals for Toddlers**...163

INTRODUCTION

You've always wanted the best for your baby. What parent wouldn't?

The food you choose for your baby can be just as important as the quality of her car seat and the safety of his crib. The healthy food choices you make for your little ones *today* will help them make healthy food choices for their entire lives. Strong immune systems, well-balanced diets, and long lives all start with *you*.

Lucky for you and your little one, feeding your baby the freshest, most wholesome food on earth is easy—and inexpensive.

First, organic food is everywhere! Nature has provided everything you need to make homemade baby food, and the modern world is finally on board. You can find organic foods in your local supermarkets, at farm stands across the country, or maybe as close as your backyard garden! Organic growers care enough to feed their animals a healthy diet and use safe methods for preparing their crops, all in an effort to promote a healthier world.

Second, making your own homemade baby food is an especially rewarding experience. You already know how great it is to cook a healthy, natural meal for yourself, but giving your baby the same quality food will make you breathe so much easier! You will choose every pea and apple that your baby eats—and you'll know *exactly* where it comes from.

And making purées for your baby is shockingly simple. You don't need to be a chef, and you don't need to buy expensive contraptions. You will succeed with determination, a blender, and this book in your hand! You can make small dinners to last a week or big batches for the freezer that last up to eight weeks.

Let's not forget about the financial benefits of making your own organic baby food. For example, one six-ounce jar of organic puréed bananas may cost around the same price as a pound of organic bananas. Where you'd get one jar of food before, you'll get six to eight by making your own!

When you make your own organic baby purées, you'll say goodbye to long receipts and limited choices. You'll have creative control of every ingredient, texture, and taste your baby experiences without limiting her food world to what is sealed in vacuum-packed glass jars.

This book highlights the importance of feeding your family organic foods and explains the whole organic process from farm to table. Each recipe features ingredients readily found in organic sections of supermarkets and grocery stores.

Because healthy eating habits start early, it's important to introduce a variety of foods, tastes, and textures during the first few years, even if it's a food you don't particularly care for yourself. One way to contribute to a picky toddler is by not consistently offering a variety of foods. If your baby doesn't seem to take a liking to certain foods at first, offer the food again at another time, but don't ban it altogether! Their taste buds will adjust and they'll become well-rounded organic connoisseurs.

QUICK REFERENCE FOR RECIPES

There are so many things to consider when purchasing foods and making purées for your baby: What foods can I freeze? Do I need to cook these peaches before puréeing? Which foods provide the most nutrition? Can I cook foods that will satisfy the baby and the rest of the family at once?

This book takes all the guesswork out of making purées by giving you those answers in the form of the following icons alongside of each recipe when applicable:

BASIC	**Basic Purée:** These recipes consist of a single ingredient and can be easily combined with other purées for a complete nutritious meal.
FREEZER	**Freezer-Friendly:** These recipes can be safely frozen for up to eight weeks.
SUPERFOOD	**Superfoods:** These recipes contain foods that are known for their powerful nutritional qualities and health benefits.
INSTANT	**Instant No-Cook Purées:** These recipes do not require cooking over heat.
PARENTS	**For Parents and Baby:** These recipes can be made along with family meals or can also be tweaked for an older person to enjoy.

Inside, you'll also find purée recipes for babies and finger foods for toddlers that can be made from meals enjoyed by the whole family, simply by taking out portions of the meal for little ones and then adding flavors and ingredients that are appropriate for older household members. In fact, you will find that many recipes, such as Cauliflower Casserole or Rotisserie Chicken Dinner, can be easily modified into a meal that's suitable for a young baby.

Are you ready to purée? Well, put on your apron, whip out your blender, and let's get started!

PART I

PURÉE PREP

Before heading to the kitchen and delving straight into the recipes there are a few things you should know about where the food should come from, its nutrition, and how you'll prepare it. Knowledge and preparation are important steps in making purées. Therefore, this part explains everything you need to know before you head out on your first shopping trip.

CHAPTER 1

ORGANICS 101
How Your Baby Benefits from Eating Organically

From the moment a child is born, she relies on her parents to give her everything she needs to develop and grow into a healthy, thriving adult. Fortunately, you can do this by providing your baby quality nutrition she needs through organic food!

The term "organic" means more to your baby than you might think. Primarily, the health benefits of feeding your baby an organic diet filled with naturally grown and raised, unprocessed foods are far superior in terms of quality, taste, and nutrition than a traditional diet made up of processed and altered foods that may contain additives, chemicals, pesticides, dyes, or artificial ingredients. Starting off with the good stuff will ensure fewer worries for you—and a cleaner bill of health for your growing baby.

In addition, your values will rub off on your child as she grows, which sets up a lifetime of good food choices and good health for future generations (and the environment, too)! Babies don't know what's good for them; they only know what they are exposed to. Therefore, if you expose your child to junk and fast foods, she'll quickly learn how good it tastes but won't understand those things are bad for her health. It's better to limit your child's knowledge to foods that only nature has provided. Offer healthy food choices and remember that you are in charge!

Here you'll get a crash course on the meaning of organic and why it's important. You'll learn about organic farming and food production, organic standards, and how this all impacts your growing baby's health.

BEGIN WITH ORGANIC FOR THE BEST START

When your baby eats a diet made up of mostly organic food, she is at less risk of developing certain diseases, neurological disorders, or other adverse health effects from chemical exposure. The United States Environmental Protection Agency (EPA) states that infants and children are at greater risks of pesticide exposure for a variety of reasons, including the following:

- They have immature or underdeveloped internal organs;
- They consume more food and water than adults, possibly increasing their exposure to pesticides in food and water;
- They play on floors or lawns or put objects in their mouths, increasing exposure to pesticides used in homes and yards.

According to the EPA, "Children's internal organs are still developing and maturing and their enzymatic, metabolic, and immune systems may provide less natural protection than those of an adult. There are 'critical periods' in human development when exposure to a toxin can permanently alter the way an individual's biological system operates. Children may be exposed more to certain pesticides because often they eat different foods than adults."

Contrary to popular belief, rinsing foods and vegetables with a mild soap solution or vegetable wash, or soaking leafy greens such as collard greens and spinach for hours, is not enough to eliminate all the pesticide residue. The only way to be sure there is no pesticide residue is to purchase organic foods, which are pesticide and chemical free!

Organic foods are the top choice for your baby to protect her health, the environment, and future generations from disease and illness.

WHAT DOES ORGANIC MEAN?

According to the United States Department of Agriculture (USDA), *organic* refers to the way farmers grow and produce agricultural products such as fruits, vegetables, livestock, dairy products, and grains. Organic food is raised in harmony with nature—it has freedom to grow without chemical intervention or genetic modification. Organic farmers are committed to maintaining their produce and livestock using natural, chemical-free methods for feeding, fertilizing, pest control, and soil maintenance. As a result, these organic methods promote healthy air, water, and soil, creating a healthier environment overall for living things.

For your baby, this sets up a beautiful foundation to help him build healthy and sustainable eating habits essential for good health, happiness, and safety. An added bonus: by keeping fresh organic produce readily available in your refrigerator and on your counters, you can decrease your son's risk of childhood obesity while keeping your own figure in check. You'll be less inclined to grab those honey buns when there are fresh organic strawberries and whipped cream in the fridge, and, as your baby gets older, he'll opt for berries instead of honey buns!

Your baby's growing body needs a variety of wholesome, nutritious foods to support good health, which is the reason to start off with organic purées. Chemicals—in the form of added artificial flavorings, dyes, pesticide and herbicide residues, and synthetic hormones—certainly do not fit into that equation and can pose dangerous health risks over time. Babies and children who are fed organic foods have limited exposure to toxins that can cause adverse neurological and behavioral effects.

LOOK AT THE LABEL

The United States Department of Agriculture (USDA) oversees the National Organic Program in accordance with the Organic Foods Production Act of 1990, which regulates under federal law the production of organic food. The USDA certifies organic producers who must follow the guidelines set forth in order to receive the organic seal of approval. This round seal, displayed with the words "USDA ORGANIC" in big bold letters, lets consumers know the product is free from antibiotics, bioengineering, irradiation, hormones, and pesticides. When you see this label, you can rest assured knowing you are providing your baby the best purée ingredients available!

There are four levels to the USDA organic labeling program:

- Products that are 100 percent organic are made entirely from organic ingredients or components and may display the "USDA Organic" seal along with the percentage.
- Products that are made up of at least 95 percent organic ingredients or components, and have remaining ingredients that are approved for use in organic products, can display the "USDA Organic" seal.
- Products that are made up of at least 70 percent organic ingredients or components can list up to three organic ingredients or food groups in the primary display panel with the word "organic" before those ingredients and **cannot** display the "USDA Organic" seal.
- Products that are made up of ingredients less than 70 percent organic cannot display the "USDA Organic" seal or list the word "organic" anywhere on the principal display. However, these manufacturers can specify "organically produced" on the ingredients statement on the information panel.

It may seem like a maze, but knowing the formula behind the labeling program will help you determine which foods are best suited for feeding your baby.

ORGANIC AND THE LITTLE GUYS

There is one caveat to the USDA's organic certification. Farmers whose sales are $5,000 or less annually are exempt from certification but must still meet organic standards in order to claim their foods are organic. Small farmers may obtain a Certified Naturally Grown (CNG) certification, which is the grassroots alternative to the USDA's certified organic program. The CNG growing standards and requirements are on par with the USDA's standards; however, the cost is more affordable to small farmers.

DON'T MISTAKE ALL-NATURAL FOR ORGANIC

You've probably seen products with labels that read "Natural," "All-Natural," "Free-Range," or "Hormone-Free" in big bold print. Many companies use these words to market their products, but **do not take their word for it** that a product is organic unless you see the proof. Always look for the USDA Organic seal unless you are purchasing food from a small farmer or producer. In that case, if possible, talk to the farmer directly about his growing methods. The main difference between "natural" and "organic" foods is that organic food production is heavily regulated and certified by the government. Natural foods are not regulated and can be labeled as such without penalty.

THE SCOOP ON GENETICALLY MODIFIED FOODS

Who ever thought the day would come when scientists would be able to extract certain genes from one species and transfer those genes into another species? Well, it's here! The process is called *genetic modification*, and genetically modified foods (commonly referred to as GM foods or GMOs, for genetically modified organisms) are showing up in grocery stores everywhere. Many people are consuming genetically modified products and don't even realize it! According to the USDA, soybeans and cotton genetically engineered with herbicide-tolerant traits have been the most widely and rapidly adopted crops in the United States, followed by insect-resistant cotton and corn.

There is great debate over whether GMO foods are safe for plants, animals, humans, or the environment. Currently, the long-term effects of consuming GMO foods is unproven so there is not enough research to support transparency in labeling or pulling it from market shelves. But GMO food labeling has been in place in Europe and Japan for years. One way to be absolutely sure you are purchasing food that has not been genetically modified is to look for the 100% USDA Certified Organic seal on the label. For more detailed information, visit *www.ers.usda.gov/Data/BiotechCrops* or *www.who.int/foodsafety/publications/biotech/20questions/en/*.

THE TOXIC TWENTY

If organic foods are out of reach or you see a deal on conventional strawberries that seems too good to pass up, consider the pesticide load—the amount of pesticides used on a crop—when you make your decision. Knowing this information before making a purchase may prompt you to say, "Thanks, but no thanks." The Environmental Working Group ranks produce based on its pesticide load. The fruits and vegetables at the top of the following list carry the heaviest load of pesticides when produced conventionally; therefore, be sure to **always** purchase these items organic. (To help you remember, these fruits and vegetables are bolded in the ingredient lists in the recipes in Part II.) Other foods such as onions or bananas, which do not carry a high level of pesticides, are safer to purchase nonorganic. To view and download the complete list, visit the Environmental Working Group's website, *www.foodnews.org*.

THE TOXIC TWENTY

1. Celery
2. Peaches
3. Strawberries
4. Apples
5. Blueberries (domestic)
6. Nectarines
7. Sweet bell peppers
8. Spinach
9. Cherries
10. Kale/collard greens
11. Potatoes
12. Grapes (imported)
13. Lettuce
14. Blueberries (imported)
15. Carrots
16. Green beans (domestic)
17. Pears
18. Plums (imported)
19. Summer squash
20. Cucumbers (imported)

Always thoroughly wash fruit and vegetables before eating them, including lemons and oranges, especially if you plan on using the skins for zest. Soaking and rinsing fresh produce in a water bath works the best to remove the dirt.

The information presented so far is not intended to scare you but to provide you with enough knowledge in order to make an informed decision as it relates to feeding your baby. Organic food is the ultimate choice that gets a five-star rating in providing the healthiest nutrition for your baby as well as your family. But wait, there is more! Organic food is not the only choice that gets a five-star rating. Certain types of food contain disease-fighting and illness-preventing nutrients and antioxidants that work miraculously to keep babies' bodies healthy. They're called superfoods!

SUPERFOODS TO THE RESCUE

Superfoods have amazing health benefits that can lead to a happy and long, healthy life. Although all foods have nutritional benefits, superfoods provide more than just nutrition. They come with incredible medical benefits. For years, superfoods have reigned supreme for improved body functioning and disease prevention and have been known to:

- Protect against cancer and heart disease
- Protect the body from harmful toxins
- Promote digestive health
- Lower blood pressure and cholesterol
- Regulate metabolism
- Promote healthy blood sugar levels
- Reduce or prevent inflammation

Superfoods are nutrient-dense, meaning they have an abundance of nutrients without a lot of empty calories. When you incorporate superfoods into purées, you'll know that every bite counts toward a healthy life. Remember to look for the superfoods symbol **SUPERFOOD** throughout this book when looking for recipes that contain these amazing ingredients.

ANTIOXIDANTS

Many superfoods are chock full of antioxidants that are essential for protecting our bodies against illness and such diseases as cancer or heart disease. Antioxidants work to counteract potential damage from free radicals, harmful molecules that cause illness and disease in our bodies. According to an article on WebMD called "Antioxidants and Your Immune System: Super Foods for Optimal Health," our bodies simply do not produce enough antioxidants needed to fight off infection. Because environmental toxins are at an all-time high, we need to consume more antioxidants than ever before to stay healthy.

HOW ANTIOXIDANTS WORK

Antioxidants consist of vitamins A, C, and E; minerals such as iron, zinc, copper, selenium, and beta-carotene; and flavonoids. Flavonoids are the biggest class of antioxidants and consist of healthy nutrients and chemicals found in plants. When you consume a variety of fruits and vegetables, your body will build up an entire defense team that works against the free radicals, keeping your body free from illness and disease. That's why it is so important to provide your baby a variety of foods to ensure he is getting an abundance of antioxidants.

SUPERFOOD HEROES

The following list represents the top fifteen superfoods that provide the highest level of antioxidants and nutrition.

SUPERFOOD HEROES
AVOCADOS
A little bit of avocado goes a long way when it comes to the antioxidant lutein that it provides. Lutein promotes good skin and healthy eye function. Your baby only needs a couple of tablespoons per serving to benefit from this superfood. Avocados are packed with protein and contain monounsaturated fat, which may help reduce his risk of diabetes, heart disease, and cancer. Serve a little mashed avocado to boost the nutrition of any meal.
BANANAS
Babies go wild for banana purées because they are smooth and sweet, but bananas also provide potassium and the carbohydrates needed for energy. Bananas are rich in fiber, which supports healthy digestion. They're easy to mash and mix in with other purées for a nutritional bonus.
BEANS
Beans are full of fiber, calcium, and protein and help prevent heart disease and support healthy cholesterol. Beans are inexpensive, yet rich in flavor and nutritional content. Incorporate beans such as black beans and pinto beans into vegetable purées, dips, and soups.
BERRIES
Most berries are not only big on flavor, they are also big on fiber, vitamins A and C, and other powerful antioxidants. Blueberries are the mightiest superhero of all the berries, as they provide the highest amount of antioxidants. Raspberries and strawberries are filled with antioxidants that boost the immune system, while cranberries are well-known for promoting a healthy urinary tract. Berries make great purées, finger foods, and of course make a great addition to muffins!

BROCCOLI

Broccoli boosts cancer prevention due to its high phytochemical content. Broccoli provides fiber, folate, calcium, beta-carotene, and vitamin C. Broccoli may appeal more to your baby when combined with other purées such as chicken, beef, or other vegetables.

BUTTERNUT SQUASH

Babies love the mild taste of butternut squash, but you'll love the super antioxidant, beta-carotene, it provides. Butternut squash also packs a powerful punch of vitamin C, fiber, folate, essential B vitamins, and potassium. Beta-carotene is known to help prevent certain types of cancer.

CARROTS

Extra rich in beta-carotene, which converts to vitamin A, this superfood hero supports healthy vision and growth. Babies love the sweet taste of carrot purée, made more vibrant and sweet when mixed with sweet potatoes, another superfood hero.

CEREAL

Iron-fortified infant cereal is an excellent source of iron for your baby for healthy brain development and growth. At around six months old, the iron stores your baby was born with start running out, and it's essential to replace those stores by serving foods rich in iron. Infant cereal is a common first food, recommended by experts because of its hypoallergenic qualities. Infant cereal is a great thickener for runny purées, and it also adds a nutritional boost.

EGGS

The zinc, choline, and vitamins A, D, E, and B_{12} that eggs provide make for a wonderful superfood for baby. Eggs are also an excellent source of protein. Recent studies from experts show that eggs can be introduced to babies as early as eight months old and should only be delayed in families with a history of food allergies. This means that your baby can benefit from their nutritional goodness sooner than later. Be sure to shop for organic eggs, and if you can afford it, free-range organic eggs are even better!

FISH

This superfood hero contains protein and omega-3 fatty acids that are important for healthy brain development and growth. Salmon is filled with DHA (docosahexaenoic acid), an omega-3 fatty acid that supports a healthy immune system, brain, and eye development. Haddock, cod, and tilapia are other great choices for introducing your baby to fish. However, because fish can be allergenic, make sure to check with your pediatrician to get the seal of approval before adding fish to your baby's diet.

SWEET POTATOES

The nutritional qualities of sweet potatoes are superior to white potatoes. Sweet potatoes are an excellent source of fiber, potassium, vitamin C, and the antioxidant beta-carotene. Sweet potatoes also contain slow-release carbohydrates for sustained energy.

RED MEAT

Red meat provides the much-needed iron that babies need for healthy brain development. Iron helps deliver red blood cells throughout the body and is considered a key nutrient that babies six months and up need the most.

TOMATOES

These red jewels are rich in the antioxidant lycopene, which helps prevent cancer and heart disease. Tomatoes can be added to many purées for a nutritional boost and for an amazing sauce for pasta and beef.

WHOLE GRAINS

Whole grains in the form of brown rice, whole-wheat flour, barley, quinoa, and oatmeal are excellent choices for your baby. Whole grains are known for decreasing the risk of heart disease by promoting healthy cholesterol levels and blood pressure. Whole grains can help reduce obesity by supporting a healthy weight in children. Whole grains are also known to promote healthy blood sugar levels and are a great source of fiber, iron, magnesium, vitamin E, and B vitamins.

YOGURT

Yogurt provides the calcium, protein, and phosphorus your baby needs to build strong bones and teeth. Yogurt comes in many varieties and endless flavors, but the most suited for babies is the full-fat variety especially made for babies. The good bacteria, known as probiotics, found in yogurt aids in healthy digestion and supports the immune system. Mix yogurt with fresh blueberry or cranberry purée for a heroic meal.

GO ORGANIC FOR THE WHOLE FAMILY

Since you're already on your way to giving your baby a healthy start, why not make a permanent lifestyle choice for everyone in the family? Maybe you're already on board with providing your family with the healthiest food on earth, which means you shop organically and provide your family with quality nutrition every day. If so, kudos to you! One of the joys of parenthood is the positive change that a new life can bring into your world. It's important to set the record straight and lead by example. After all, your baby will be watching you—imitating everything you say and do. She'll want to be just like you! Get the whole family on board and introduce everyone to organic food. Let them know this is how you'll all be eating from now on because it's better for everyone *and* you need to set a good example for the baby!

Now that you've learned about the amazing health benefits that superfoods offer, it's important to offer your baby and family a colorful assortment of fruits and vegetables at every meal. The *Dietary Guidelines for Americans*, as put forth by the federal government, suggests especially increasing the intake of dark green, red, and orange vegetables, as well as beans and peas. Fortunately, these recommendations are easy to follow because these foods are readily accessible. Just venture outside your door and get ready to go on an organic shopping crusade!

CHAPTER 2

ORGANIC MADE ACCESSIBLE
Stocking Your Pure Food Pantry

Now that you're sold on why it makes sense to eat organically, you need to know where to get it. More and more, you'll find organic food everywhere! Many of your local supermarkets carry fresh, frozen, and canned organic foods, giving you plenty of options. In addition, many large grocery chains and health food stores solely offer organic foods and products that promote excellent health. However, one of the best places to procure fresh organic fruit and vegetables is directly from the organic farmer who may be stationed at your local farmers' market, at a farm stand on the corner, or right in your neighborhood! When you visit the farmer, you're going directly to the source. The only thing standing between you and the farmer are many bushels or acres of fresh organic produce that awaits.

Although organic food is usually more expensive than conventional foods because of the laborious efforts of organic farmers, the health benefits from keeping man-made chemicals out of your body are well worth the relatively small expense. When you factor in the fact that a healthy body means fewer trips to the doctor or hospital, you could very possibly save thousands of dollars in the long term. Also, when you consider the money paid through tax dollars for environmental cleanup of pollution, the cost of growing and procuring organic food doesn't seem so hefty after all.

When getting ready to stock your pantry with foods to make baby purées, you'll find that you have many organic options right at your fingertips, including fresh, frozen, and canned foods.

CHOOSING BETWEEN FRESH, FROZEN, OR CANNED

Decisions . . . decisions. Deciding whether to choose fresh, frozen, or canned food depends on when you plan to make purées for your baby and other nutritional factors. Fresh fruit and vegetables are the top choice if you plan to purée food for your baby within a day or two of purchase. However, keep in mind that imported produce is picked several days before it makes its way to the grocery store and likely sits in produce bins for several days before you arrive to shop. Therefore, subject everything you select to close scrutiny— make sure the melons are fragrant but firm, strawberries are plump and free from mold, and the beans look bright!

FRESH FROM THE FARM

An excellent option for purchasing fresh produce is at your local farmers' market or farm stand. The food contains more nutrients because it doesn't travel far (once produce is harvested, it loses vitamins and nutrients over time). Some farms even let you pick your own, which means you can take home an organic harvest straight from the source. It's a great experience for the entire family, and nothing's fresher than picking a bushel of apples off the tree yourself, like back in the old days. To find a list of farms in your area that offer this, visit *www.pickyourown.org*.

Another option for procuring fresh organic produce is through community-supported agriculture (CSA) that many farms offer. In a CSA, the consumer helps support the costs of growing the fruits and vegetables by purchasing a "share" or membership in the CSA and then pays either by the week, month, or growing season in order to receive a weekly box of fresh fruits and vegetables straight from the farm. This box includes a variety of fruits, vegetables, or other farm products such as eggs and bread. Some CSAs even allow you to mix and match and make your own choices according to your preferences. What you end up with is more produce than you know what to do with—for little money!

The CSA model helps many small farmers to continue to farm, and revenue earned from the membership or share fees goes toward buying seed and the initial costs of planting, so the farmer does not have to wait for the harvest to collect money. This model allows the consumer to become directly involved in the food-production process. To learn more about community-supported agriculture and how you can become involved, visit *www .localharvest.org.*

FRESH FROM YOUR BACKYARD

Another option is to make purées using fresh produce found outside your door! Your own backyard or patio provides ample space and opportunity to grow organic produce. A small garden plot or a few containers are sufficient for a continuous harvest of herbs and other vegetables. This can be an inexpensive option to ensure that the organic tomatoes you love are just a few steps away. Designating a small garden plot in your backyard can create an abundance of salad greens, root vegetables, and herbs. It's important to purchase organic seeds, soil, fertilizer, and pest control (or make your own). You may have to remedy past soil contamination problems, but don't let that stop you from making the effort. There's no shortage of resources to help home gardeners. A great place to start is by visiting *www.organic homegardener.com* and picking up a copy of *Organic Gardener* magazine. Also look to your local gardening center to help you achieve the goal of growing organic food to serve your family.

If time or knowledge on the subject are in short supply, there are also companies in some areas that will install a raised organic garden bed for you. The upfront expenses may seem high, but over time the harvest will pay for itself as long as you commit to growing your own produce—which is never a bad idea!

WHEN TO CHOOSE FROZEN FOOD

Frozen foods are a great choice for making purées without worrying about your produce quickly going bad. It's easy to stockpile your freezer with a variety of fruit and veggies, especially varieties that are out of season. That way your baby can enjoy the tastes of all seasons and you can save yourself from making extra trips to the store. Also, if the fresh produce in the grocery store looks shabby, purchasing frozen food would be a superior choice. Frozen foods are harvested and flash frozen within six hours; therefore, many of the nutrients are well retained and may even have more of certain vitamins than fresh food does near the end of its life.

For the most part, frozen foods also keep their flavor, but the subtle difference will be unnoticeable to your baby. A few national organic brands include 365 Organic Everyday Value (sold at Whole Foods), Woodstock Farms, Stoneyfield Farm, and Cascadian Farm.

WHEN CANNED FOODS ARE BEST

It's always a great idea to have canned foods on hand for convenience and in the event of an emergency. However, there is evidence that show canned foods and some packaged foods are exposed to bisphenol A (BPA), a toxic, unregulated chemical used to line metal food and drink cans (including formula cans) and type #7 polycarbonate (PC) plastics. BPA is harmful to humans, even in low doses, and can cause serious health problems and diseases. Make sure the cans you purchase are BPA free. If you are uncertain, contact the company directly to be sure. A consumer-supported list for companies that use or have banned BPA can be found at *www.organicgrace.com/node/316*. For more information on BPA, visit the Environmental Working Group's website at *www.ewg.org/reports/bisphenola*.

Because purées are frozen or refrigerated, they are susceptible to spoiling when the refrigerator breaks down, there is a power outage, or other disaster. It's best to be prepared because you never know what mother nature has in store. For this reason, always keep an emergency stash of canned goods such as pears, green beans, corn, carrots, yams, and infant formula in your pantry. Canned beans, fruits, and vegetables are a good source of nutrition and can easily be prepared for the family and fork puréed for baby in the event of an emergency. You might also consider having a day's worth of prepackaged organic baby food in your diaper bag, just in case you get stuck with a flat tire or the visit to your mother-in-law's turns into a sleepover!

These days, busy moms and dads don't have time to slave over the stove stewing tomatoes or preparing beans. Fortunately, these items are best purchased in cans. Canned beans are an excellent source of protein, iron, and fiber, and they are easy to prepare—just open up the can and cook 'em! Tomato sauces and tomatoes are the number one choice for canned foods because they provide lycopene, an antioxidant that aids in cancer prevention. Research shows that lycopene is easily absorbed into the body because of the heat from the canning process. Therefore, purchase canned organic tomatoes and sauces to incorporate into baby purées. Make sure they are 100 percent plain tomatoes of any variety (diced, stewed, sauces, etc.) with no added sugar, spices, or other ingredients.

Pumpkin is another staple in canned goods. Cooking pie pumpkins or the big pumpkins can eat up precious time that you may not have. Therefore, pure canned pumpkin is great for incorporating in purées, muffins, yogurt, or pudding. Take care not to get pumpkin pie filling, as it contains lots of sugar and is primarily used for baking pies. While you're out on your shopping adventure, scour the aisles to see what is offered. However, remember that canned foods, whether for babies or not, have been produced to last for years. Commercially canned food is heated to extreme temperatures and then cooled, which destroys many of the nutrients, and the taste doesn't come close to fresh. Purchase canned or jarred food, with the exception of the tomatoes, beans, and pumpkin, as a last resort or to add to your emergency food supply.

PANTRY FOR PURÉES

It's good to keep a well-stocked kitchen filled with staples and commonly used items in your refrigerator and pantry. Serve seasonal foods in all colors along with an array of whole grains and proteins to ensure your baby receives a well-balanced diet. Here are some suggestions for foods to keep on hand to make purées and finger food *and* foods to keep on hand in an emergency situation. Stocking your pantry with these organic staples will allow you to whip up a variety of meals in a pinch!

FRESH PRODUCE (FOR QUICK AND EASY FRESH PURÉES)				
bananas	apples	pears	sweet potatoes	squash
mangoes	avocados			

FROZEN FOODS (TO INTRODUCE TO YOUR FREEZER STASH)				
broccoli	cauliflower	green beans	peas	peaches
blueberries	chicken	fish	beef	

CANNED FOODS (MAKE GREAT EMERGENCY ITEMS)		
tomatoes and sauces	beans (black, pinto, kidney, cannellini)	plain pumpkin
green beans	corn	yams
tuna	fruit	

SEASONINGS			
ground cinnamon	nutmeg	thyme	dill
paprika	ginger	garlic powder	

HERBS (IDEALLY FRESH, BUT DRIED HERBS WORK AS WELL)				
mint	parsley	oregano	bay leaves	dill

STOCKS (LOW-SODIUM VARIETIES OR HOMEMADE)
chicken, beef, and vegetable

OILS		
olive oil	canola oil	sesame oil

DAIRY AND EGGS		
eggs (choose medium or large organic eggs)	cheese (mild Cheddar, Parmesan, fontina, and cream cheese)	yogurt (full-fat yogurt is needed for babies under two years old)
butter (choose unsalted)	milk (whole cow's milk, goat's milk, soy, or rice milk)	

STAPLE PRODUCTS	
pasta (mini spaghetti, farfalle, rotini, shells, or pasta stars)	rice (arborio rice, wild rice, white and brown long-grain)
beans and legumes (black beans, pinto beans, lentils, and split peas)	cereals (infant cereals, oatmeal, grits, granola, and muesli)

WHEN ORGANIC FOODS ARE OUT OF REACH

Organic food can be found more readily than in previous years because more people are requesting organics and the stores are catering to the demand. However, there may be times when the particular food you are looking for is not available or falls outside of your budget. Here you'll learn how to save on organic groceries and the top twenty foods to purchase organic.

SAVE ON YOUR ORGANIC GROCERY BILL

Although providing your baby with a completely organic diet is ideal, the slightly higher price tag that comes with purchasing organic food is often not ideal. However, keep in mind that *raw* organic ingredients are still less expensive than buying the itty bitty jars and packages of processed baby food—whether you opt for organic or not! This means that when you make your own baby food you are still in the black. Recent studies show that consumers will pay 21 cents more per container of commercial brands of organic baby food. That means you pay more than a dollar for every five servings, which can add up to around thirty dollars extra per month. That savings alone may be enough to purchase raw organic ingredients to last at least two months. Just imagine how much fresh organic produce you can buy for thirty dollars! Remember that companies are in business to make a profit. Some of the major brands spend big money on the cost of manufacturing and marketing. Those expenses are passed onto you, the consumer, who pays for small containers of food that, although nutritious, don't taste that great or stretch your dollar. What you end up with is either a bunch of tiny glass jars that you don't know how to reuse (and eventually end up in the trash) or a bunch of plastic containers and packages that clutter the landfills and smother the earth. With that said, the cost of organic food may not seem so expensive after all.

Other ways to trim off your family's grocery budget to ensure a continuous supply of organic foods are as follows:

1. *Clip coupons*: Collect newspapers and circulars and use coupons to save money on groceries and other household items you normally buy, such as toothpaste and laundry detergent. It's amazing how much you can save with a little planning and a pair of scissors.
2. *Buy less processed food*: Shop on the outer perimeter of the store and purchase less convenient foods, which usually costs more than making the same dish from scratch. Examine your grocery cart before you check out and make sure you aren't double buying. For example, you may have a bag of fresh potatoes in your cart and a bag of frozen French fries. Use the fresh potatoes to make homemade French fries and put the frozen fries back. That alone will save a few dollars!

3. *Grown your own*: Planting a garden is an inexpensive way to provide fresh organic produce for your dinner table. Many vegetables and berries can be grown with little effort in your backyard or even in containers on a small balcony or patio.

4. *Buy in bulk*: A clever way to get the most for your money is to purchase fresh produce in bulk, where the more you buy the more you save. If you don't want or need a lot, share the cost with a friend or neighbor and split the harvest. Many warehouse stores, which require membership, offer fresh organic produce at cheaper prices than smaller stores.

5. *Get the most out of the season*: Fresh produce in season is usually a lot less expensive than foods that are not in season. Stock up on these goodies and purée and freeze the extra to extend the season and save money by not purchasing at the higher out-of-season price later on.

Once you get in the habit of shopping organically, it will become second nature and you won't think twice about it. You'll find that you *can* have the organic foods that you need for your baby and are actually under budget because of the savings from not purchasing packaged baby purées off the shelf.

Next you'll learn how to turn your brilliantly colorful organic pantry into delicious homemade meals for baby (and family). Let's explore how to equip your kitchen with the gadgets you need, safety in the kitchen, and how to purée!

SQUASH AND CORN COMBO

PAPAYA-PEAR OATMEAL

POPEYE'S
SPINACH
MEAL

SUMMER-
TIME
PEACH
RASPBERRY
DELIGHT

BLUEBERRY
MINI
MUFFINS

BANANA
BLUEBERRY
BUCKLE

THE TOXIC TWENTY

Remember, according to the Environmental Working Group, these twenty ingredients are most likely to carry heavy loads of pesticides. Whenever you can, look for organic varieties of these fruits and vegetables! You can find a complete list at *www.foodnews.org*.

CELERY

PEACHES

STRAWBERRIES

APPLES

BLUEBERRIES
(domestic and imported)

NECTARINES

SWEET BELL PEPPERS

SPINACH

CHERRIES

KALE

COLLARD GREENS

POTATOES

GRAPES (imported)

LETTUCE

CARROTS

GREEN BEANS (domestic)

PEARS

PLUMS (imported)

SUMMER SQUASH

CUCUMBERS (imported)

FRESH STRAWBERRY
YOGURT

GARLIC ASPARAGUS
WITH PARMESAN

JARS

LABELS

Banana

ICE CUBE
TRAYS

FREEZER BAGS

CHAPTER 3

BABY PURÉE ESSENTIALS
Tips, Tricks, and Techniques for Healthy Homemade Meals

When your baby has reached six months of age, you can safely introduce solid foods as long as she is showing signs she is ready and you have already discussed starting solids with your pediatrician. Cooking meals for your baby is easy, fun, and rewarding. In this chapter you'll find the tools you need to get started, the requisites of food safety, and how to prepare and store baby purées. You'll learn all about making large quantities to freeze for later use and how to make the consistency perfect for your baby at each developmental stage.

EQUIPPED, ARMED, AND PREPARED!

If you go into any kitchen supply store, you will find a gadget for everything, which can add up really quickly if you try to buy it all! Instead, save your money to purchase the organic food you need and leave the unnecessary gadgets at the store. You probably own all the things you need to make food for your baby. Not to mention, too many gadgets can overwhelm your kitchen with clutter, which will only drive you out of it. Keep your kitchen as serene as possible. Put fresh flowers out on your counter each week and maybe keep a radio or small television handy for company. Keep clutter off the counters and leave only the most commonly used *practical* items at hand. The first step to getting started making food for your little one is making sure you are relaxed and ready for this great experience! If you can't find what you did with the steaming contraption or your pantry is in chaos and you can't find the rice cereal, that's a recipe for a hot mess!

TOOLS OF THE TRADE

Here are the tools you need to get started making organic baby purées:

- Large cutting board
- Large chef's knife
- Small paring knife
- Vegetable peeler
- Wooden spoons
- Measuring cups and spoons
- Baking sheets
- Stock pot
- 2-quart saucepan
- 12-inch nonstick skillet
- Baking dishes
- Mixing bowls
- Cooling rack
- Large pot with steamer insert or collapsible steamer
- Meat thermometer
- Fine mesh stainless-steel strainer
- Blender or mini food processor
- Food mill
- Ice cube trays
- Plastic wrap
- Freezer bags
- Black permanent marker for labeling

STOCK SMART

As you can see, making and preparing healthy organic food for your baby doesn't require a large investment. You may find that you only need a few items from the list. How wonderful is that? Read on to learn about the pieces of equipment that will truly become indispensable when making organic baby food.

STEAMER BASKET

A steamer basket fits nice and snug in a medium to large pot for steaming small batches of food. Many pots and pans sets come with a steamer basket. You can also use a rice or vegetable steamer if you have one on hand.

FINE MESH STAINLESS-STEEL STRAINER

The holes in your pasta colander are too large to catch fine seeds and excess fibers that didn't get puréed enough for your infant to tolerate, but a strainer will do the trick. A stainless-steel strainer will resist rust and can last for years.

BLENDER OR MINI FOOD PROCESSOR

Any blender or food processor that has a purée function will work perfectly for making baby food purées. Blenders that have large glass pitchers are best for making large quantities and transferring hot liquids and food. Be sure that you have enough capacity for the amount of baby food you intend to make. Blenders are more practical because they can stay out on your counter, making it easy to whip up baby food without bringing out an extra appliance. A mini food processor is good for grinding up grains for cereals, nuts, or other hard foods.

HANDHELD BLENDER

A handheld blender makes it easy to purée small meals in their own containers. Some also come with attachable containers that allow them to serve the same function as a mini food processor as well!

FOOD MILL

Food mills are great for puréeing foods with skins or husks such as corn, blueberries, and green beans for young babies. All the food will get mashed, but the indigestible portion stays on the top.

ICE CUBE TRAYS

Ice cube trays are handy for freezing purées into small portions that can be used later. Once frozen, you pop them out and into storage bags for your freezer. Each ice cube–sized portion is equivalent to 2 tablespoons or about 1 ounce. The cubes can easily be mixed together, and you can grab as many as you need to make your desired portion. The best part about using ice cube trays is that they stack, they don't take up a lot of freezer space, and they are so inexpensive you can buy as many as you need for the amount of food you want to make. Be sure to label and date the storage bags so you know how long your purées have been in the freezer.

In addition to these items, of course, you'll need feeding supplies for your little one. Keep a few bibs, small bowls, and baby spoons handy to start off. As your baby starts to self-feed, you can upgrade to plates with dividers and forks. Many stores offer melamine bowls and plates for children. Melamine is *not* microwave safe, so take care to always heat your baby's food in a glass dish and transfer the food to your child's plate.

If your budget allows, invest in a highchair that your baby can use until well after his first year. The best highchairs are the ones that can be strapped around a dining room chair so that it doesn't take up additional space. Some highchairs make it difficult for a baby to sit at the table in small living quarters, and it's important that your baby share meals with you and the rest of the family. This will help establish a healthy eating routine at an early age.

SAFETY FIRST

In order to keep sanity in the kitchen it's important to practice safe hygiene every time you make a meal. Contaminated counters, appliances, and feeding supplies are a sure way to drive you insane—and possibly everyone you've fed to the hospital.

Safe food handling practices are a *must* for preparing baby purées or any food that you make. Follow these tips to reduce the risk of contamination and illness.

- Always wash your hands for twenty seconds with warm, soapy water before and after handling food. Make sure you clean your wrists and under your nails.
- Frequently clean the areas where you prepare food, including counters, sinks, faucets, and floors, with an eco-friendly cleaning solution.
- Separate meat and poultry from other food items.
- Wash cutting surfaces with hot soapy water after each use. Cross-contamination can occur when you place cooked meat or produce on surfaces contaminated by raw meat.

- Always cook food to proper temperatures. Use a meat thermometer to make sure meat is completely done.
- Refrigerate your food right away so bacteria cannot grow on the food. Don't let the food sit out on the counter!

Following these safety guidelines will ensure the health and safety of your family.

SAVVY COOKING TECHNIQUES

There are many ways to cook purées for your baby. Knowing the pros and cons of your appliances will help you decide which to use to cook foods thoroughly. When deciding on a cooking technique, consider the season and the reason. For example, if it's cold outside and you're swamped with things to do, consider baking. Or, if you planned on making steamed broccoli for the family, you might decide to steam apples or cauliflower for your baby while the pot is already out. The following are commonly used cooking methods for making baby purées.

BAKING

Baking retains the most nutrients but takes the longest to cook foods until tender, especially potatoes, squash, and meats. However, while the food is in the oven, you can get other things accomplished around the house. You will bake most things at 350°F, which is the most common temperature used for baking. Because of the oven's large capacity, you can bake up to four different dishes simultaneously, making it easy to prepare a couple months' worth of food. For example, you can bake sweet potatoes, squash, apples, and eggplant at the same time. If you have a double oven, you can even double that amount!

STEAMING

Steaming preserves more nutrients and antioxidants than boiling or microwaving. Therefore, it is a good way to cook fruits and vegetables. To steam using a pot and steaming basket, simply fill the pot with enough water to reach the bottom of the basket. Add the food to the basket and turn the burner on medium-high heat. You'll find that most food cooks quickly using this method. Steam until the fruit or vegetable is pierced easily with a fork.

MICROWAVING

Microwaving is quick and convenient for cooking many fruits, vegetables, and cereals. With microwave cooking, there are definite space limitations—you can only cook small batches. In addition, there's much controversy swirling around whether this method retains nutrients in food. Until there's definitive evidence, it's up to you to decide, but recent studies have shown that microwaving does destroy precious antioxidants found in food. Therefore, just like with boiling, use it as a last resort for heating foods used to make baby purées. If you are going to reheat food, reduce the power to 30 to 50 percent to reduce hot spots.

Consider these additional warnings when using the microwave. First, never heat up food in plastic dishes that are in plastic wrap or not marked "microwave safe." Research has shown that the plastic causes toxic chemicals that seep into the food and can cause long-term detrimental effects. Look on the bottom of a plastic dish to see if it is marked as microwave safe. If you are unsure, play it safe and don't use the dish in the microwave. Instead, use a glass dish. Second, never heat up food covered in aluminum foil or leave metal eating utensils in the bowl. That is a quick way to send your kitchen up in flames!

BOILING

Boiling is the least beneficial cooking method, so turn to it as a last resort. Studies show that about 50 percent of the nutrients seep into the water during the cooking process. Many people don't know this and pour the remaining nutrient-rich liquid down the drain. Now that you're equipped with this important knowledge, be sure to incorporate the remaining liquid in your purées, should you decide to use this cooking method.

IT'S ALL ABOUT CONSISTENCY

There are three types of baby purée consistencies—smooth, semismooth, and chunky.

A smooth purée is appropriate for babies just starting to eat solids, at around six months of age. Smooth purées are free of bumps, lumps, and fibrous materials. It is similar to the consistency of plain yogurt or commercial stage 1 baby food. Your blender will achieve this purée with water or other liquids added. The purée will eventually resemble a whirlpool while being processed, which is a good indicator of a smooth texture. Starchy foods such as potatoes may require lots of added water, while some foods that naturally retain water, like pears, may not need any additional liquid. Therefore, turn on the purée function first and then gradually add liquid in small quantities at a time to achieve a smooth texture.

The semismooth consistency is smooth like yogurt but has small chunks of food here and there to help babies around eight months old learn to chew. These tiny chunks of soft food can be things like rice, pasta, and diced cooked vegetables. The semismooth consistency is comparable to commercial stage 2 baby food. A good way to achieve a semismooth consistency is to add minced pieces of cooked, soft foods to a smooth purée.

The final consistency is chunky. You can achieve a chunky consistency with less puréeing, or you can also purée to a smooth consistency and then add diced chunks of fruit, vegetables, or pasta back in. A chunky consistency is comparable to commercial stage 3 baby food.

Purchasing these three stages of commercial organic baby food will give you some idea of what the purées are like at each stage. Don't be afraid to take a taste. After all, it will be a great reminder of why you are making baby food in the first place!

ACHIEVING THE PERFECT PURÉE CONSISTENCY

With your first few attempts of making purées, it is possible to make simple mistakes like adding too much liquid or not adding enough. If this happens to you, don't start over. It is not necessary to throw out the food because it is not the right consistency. Instead, try making these few minor adjustments to get the consistency just right.

- Thinning: If your purée is too thick, try thinning it out by adding cool boiled water or by using any leftover liquid from steaming or boiling. You may also use fresh breast milk or formula for an added nutritional boost. However, if you plan on freezing the purée, don't add formula or breast milk.
- Thickening: To thicken purées that are too thin, you can add more cooked food if you have more, or add infant cereal such as rice or oatmeal. However, there are other foods that can be used as thickeners such as mashed potatoes, yogurt, wheat germ, or cottage cheese. Make sure that whatever you add has already been introduced to your baby and that you do not freeze these ingredients with the purée. Use these ingredients as thickeners when you are ready to feed your baby.

It is also important to check the purée to make sure there are no unprocessed chunks. Some foods are naturally lumpy or grainy, but as long as there are no actual chunks or fibrous material, it should be safe to proceed with feeding.

PERFECTO! PURÉES STEP BY STEP

With a little planning, your time shopping and in the kitchen can go to great use, and you'll be whipping up batches of nutritious organic purées with ease! Follow these five simple steps for purée success.

STEP 1: SCHEDULE TIME

The best thought-out plan will result in a hassle- and stress-free chef . . . you! Therefore, set the time aside for grocery shopping *and* making purées for your baby each week, month, or whatever interval you choose. Don't schedule these tasks on days when you have other things to do or are pressed for time. Schedule a grocery day and a purée day separately. Shopping for the best foods will be more time-consuming than you think because you will want to find the ripest pear or the freshest bananas. Therefore, by the time you get home from shopping you may be too exhausted to prep and purée, too. But if you've got the energy and ambition, there is no point in putting off for tomorrow what you can do today!

If you have fun friends, invite them over for a purée party! Friends make the best prep and line cooks, so there's no point in doing it all by yourself. Make the time fun and dedicate the time solely for making purées for your baby.

STEP 2: GO SHOPPING

Shopping for organic food can be a great outing for everyone to enjoy. Don't forget to take your reusable shopping bags to bring home all the wonderful food you purchase. But how much should you buy? To make a big batch that will last a month or two, start out with about two pounds of foods that can be cooked and frozen such as sweet potatoes, green beans, squash, etc. For perishable foods, such as bananas and avocado, purchase a couple initially, and plan to serve those foods fresh. Plan to replenish the perishable foods as soon as they are consumed. Once you get going, you'll be able to gauge how much your baby eats and can plan your future shopping trips accordingly.

STEP 3: FOOD PREPARATION

You might want to tune in to the Food Network or gather your prep cooks for this step! Time flies when you're having fun, so preparing foods while watching Paula Deen or in harmony with your closest friends is a great way to add excitement to cooking.

Here is how you will prepare most fresh fruit and vegetables for puréeing:

1. Wash each food thoroughly. Drain on a clean kitchen towel.
2. Remove all peels, seeds, and cores.
3. Trim ends and all inedible parts (such as stems).
4. Cut into halves or quarters fruit/vegetables that will require steaming. Leave potatoes and squash in peels for baking or roasting.

STEP 4: COOK

Cook everything using your preferred cooking method, taking into account the tips in the Savvy Cooking Techniques section earlier in the chapter.

STEP 5: PURÉE AND FREEZE

Purée foods one ingredient at a time in a blender. Make sure to thoroughly wash the blender between purées. Spoon purées into ice cube trays, leaving just a little room near the top for the cube to expand once frozen. Cover with plastic wrap and freeze for twenty-four hours or until set. Remove cubes from ice cube trays and transfer to freezer-safe bags. Label and freeze for eight to twelve weeks.

Rules for Storing Purées
- Put perishable purées in the refrigerator immediately after cooking or processing.
- Cook and freeze all meat, poultry, and fish before the expiration date on the package.
- Refrigerate uncooked poultry, fish, or meat separately from fruit, vegetables, or any other raw food to prevent cross-contamination.
- Keep refrigerator set at 40°F or below, and freezer at 0°F.

FREEZING AND THAWING HOMEMADE PURÉES

Freezing your baby purées ensures that you'll have plenty of food for the coming months. A little time spent up front can mean a freezer well stocked with a variety of fruit, vegetables, and meats for up to twelve weeks! You won't spend hours in the kitchen each day or even each week. Just a few hours a month is all you need to prepare a couple of months' worth of baby food.

To get started, you'll need several ice cube trays, plastic wrap, freezer bags, and a permanent marker or label. When your purées have been cooked and cooled, spoon the mixture into the ice cube trays and repeat this process for each type of food. However, only freeze one type of food per tray. Otherwise, you may forget what you've added.

Recommendations for freezing times to maintain freshness:

- Fruit purées—up to eight weeks
- Vegetable purées—up to eight weeks
- Meat purées—up to twelve weeks

ON TO THE RECIPES!

Now that your kitchen is fully equipped, serene, and safe—and you've called all your friends and invited an Iron Chef to help out—it's time to put all of your newfound knowledge into action by experimenting with the following delicious recipes that your growing baby is sure to gobble up!

PART II

ORGANIC PURÉES FOR EACH AGE

Every baby develops at his own pace, in his own unique way. Your child will undergo rapid growth and development each month. Now is the time to take out your digital camera or camcorder to capture these precious moments. Proudly display photos of the organic purées that you make to your friends on Facebook or Flickr, and let the world see how you're raising a healthy and organic baby and inspire others to do the same! In the following chapters you'll find recipes for the four stages on the developmental ladder of feeding. Your child will acquire new skills in each stage to prepare him for the next. Food purées will go from smooth and runny to diced foods your child can pick up. Pay attention to your child's developmental stages and feed according to the skills he has.

FIRST-STAGE MEALS (SIX TO SEVEN MONTHS)
Smooth Purées for Beginner Explorers

At this point in your baby's development, there's a whole new world outside of breast milk or formula for him to explore. From six months old, your baby is now able to experience his first taste of solid food. This chapter introduces basic purées consisting of single ingredients for your baby to discover. At this stage, start off with smooth purées that run off the spoon and then gradually thicken to a yogurtlike consistency. Introduce foods one at a time, and wait four to seven days before introducing another one. If your baby displays any signs of an allergic reaction, such as rash, swelling, difficulty breathing, vomiting, or diarrhea, discontinue all foods in question and contact your family physician immediately for further instruction. Once your child has tolerated a food, try offering a new single-ingredient food and repeat the process. You can then combine foods that have been tolerated for additional flavor and texture.

Iron-fortified infant cereals such as rice, oatmeal, and barley are a great introduction to the new world of food. Babies need foods rich in iron and fat for healthy brain development. Alternatively, avocados, potatoes, yogurt, bananas, pears, and apples are popular hits among babies because of these foods' mild, sweet taste. This stage allows your baby to experience the true taste of nature without added spices or other ingredients—just simple goodness.

FIRST STAGE: SIX MONTHS

Up until six months of age, milk provides all the wholesome goodness essential for your baby's growth and development. Babies are born with enough iron stores for six months, so it's important to ensure your baby gets enough iron from baby purées and transitional food up until her second birthday. Iron deficiency runs rampant in children, and the lack of iron can cause impaired mental development. Once your baby reaches six months, she'll be eager to try solids and will probably seem interested in the foods you eat. Weaning baby from milk to solids is that first step on the developmental ladder of feeding, and a very rewarding one at that! By six months of age your baby should be able to hold her neck up and begin to sit with support. She can reach and grasp for objects, including her spoon! She's also imitating chewing by moving her jaws up and down. In addition to first-stage foods, offer your child as much breast milk as she wants or 24–32 ounces of formula per day. Here are some first foods to begin feeding your baby.

FIRST-STAGE CUISINES

- Avocados
- Apples (sweet varieties)
- Bananas
- Butternut squash
- Infant cereals (rice, oatmeal, or barley)
- Pears
- Peas
- Pumpkin
- Sweet potatoes
- White potatoes
- Yogurt (baby-specific types)

If your baby doesn't seem interested in a particular food, continue to offer the food a few days later and keep repeating this process until she accepts the new taste. She may initially take a tablespoon or so before she is satisfied; however, her appetite and interest will increase over a short period of time. After your baby has accepted the first foods, try offering more variety in the first-stage purées with the recipes featured in Chapters 4 and 5.

Homemade Rice Cereal

BASIC

Rice cereal is one of the most common first foods for babies. It is easy to digest and doesn't carry the allergenic potential of other wheat-based cereals because it is gluten free. Make enough for your little one, or prepare a larger serving for the older children!

3 SERVINGS

¼ cup white or brown rice

1 cup water

Breast milk or formula for thinning as needed

1. Grind rice into a powder, using a food processor.
2. Pour water into a small saucepan. Bring to a rolling boil.
3. Add the rice powder into the boiling water, stirring constantly for about 30 seconds.
4. Cover the pot, turn the heat down to low, and simmer for 7–8 minutes, or until the rice is a smooth, thick consistency. Stir occasionally to prevent sticking.
5. Let cool to lukewarm. Thin with breast milk or formula to desired consistency. For a baby just starting solids, the cereal should be thin and run off the spoon easily.

First Cereals

Rice, oatmeal, and barley are all excellent grains that can be prepared into cereals and introduced to your baby as early as four months old as long as she is developmentally ready. Beware, though, of cereals that may contain wheat. If your family has a history of food allergies, delay introducing wheat and get the okay from your pediatrician to be on the safe side. Also, remember that breast milk, and even organic formula, can be used to thin purées. Water can also be used, but adding the breast milk or formula will give the purée a nutritional boost.

Homemade Oatmeal Cereal

BASIC

Oatmeal is a stick-to-your-ribs type of cereal. The whole grains are excellent for baby and provide sustained energy. A note on 1-cup-water quantities: ¼ cup of oats may be difficult to purée in a full-size food processor. Use a mini grinder when making small amounts, or make a larger amount of oatmeal and store the extra. Keep it tightly sealed, and it will last for 1 to 2 weeks.

3 SERVINGS

¼ cup regular oats (not quick-cooking)

1 cup water

Breast milk or formula for thinning as needed

1. Grind oats into a powder, using a food processor or blender. Alternatively, a mortar and pestle make a terrific grinder for a small amount.

2. Bring water to a rolling boil in a small saucepan.

3. Add the powdered oats into the boiling water, stirring constantly for about 30 seconds.

4. Cover the pot, turn the heat down to low, and simmer for 8–10 minutes, or until the oats are smooth and thick. Stir occasionally to prevent sticking and burning.

5. Let cool to lukewarm. Thin if desired.

Homemade Barley Cereal

BASIC

Barley has a slightly stronger flavor than rice or oatmeal. For this reason, try introducing it after your baby is already accustomed to other cereals.

3 SERVINGS

¼ cup barley

1 cup water

Breast milk or water for thinning as needed

1. Grind barley into a powder, using either a food processor or coffee bean grinder.

2. Pour water into a small saucepan. Bring to a rolling boil.

3. Add ground barley into the boiling water, stirring constantly for about 30 seconds.

4. Cover the pot, turn the heat down to low, and simmer for 8–10 minutes. Stir to prevent sticking.

5. Let cool to lukewarm. Thin until smooth.

Enchanting Apple

BASIC/FREEZER

Golden Delicious, Braeburn, and Gala apples make particularly good apple purée, though almost any variety can be used.

10–12 SERVINGS

4 medium apples, peeled, cored, and chopped (variety of your choice)

2 tablespoons water

1. In a medium-sized pan, combine apples and 2 tablespoons water.
2. Cover and cook on low heat for about 10 minutes until tender.
3. Transfer all ingredients to blender and purée until desired consistency is reached.

Pretty Peas

BASIC/FREEZER/PARENTS

Sweet peas burst with flavor and add a nice touch to meat purées or other vegetables such as carrots, cauliflower, and potatoes. Sweet peas are a great introduction to solids foods and will have your child saying "pretty peas" for more!

4 SERVINGS

1 cup frozen or fresh sweet peas

½ cup water

1. Put the peas into a steamer basket, or place into a saucepan covered by 1 inch of water. Steam the peas until tender, about 10–12 minutes. Reserve water.
2. Transfer peas to blender using a slotted spoon.
3. Purée peas while gradually adding just enough of the reserved water to reach a smooth consistency.

Simply Sweet Potato

Sweet potatoes are packed with antioxidants and are easy for most babies to digest. When baked, you can quickly purée by mashing with a fork instead of using a blender. Keep plenty of these carotene-rich wonders on hand; they'll last longer than fruit and other vegetables.

8–10 SERVINGS

2 large sweet potatoes

2 cups cooled, boiled water

1. Bake sweet potatoes on a baking sheet at 350°F for about 45 minutes or until potatoes start to pucker. Let stand for 15 minutes.

2. Slice each potato in half and scoop out flesh into blender.

3. Purée while gradually adding just enough water to reach a smooth consistency. Freeze extra portions for up to eight weeks.

Blushing Bananas

Use bananas that have started spotting with brown spots because they are ripe and easy to mash. Use the other half of the banana to enjoy for yourself.

1 SERVING

½ large ripe banana

1. Cut banana in half and peel one half, removing any strings.

2. Place banana flesh in bowl.

3. Mash with a fork until smooth and creamy.

Avocado Mash

BASIC/SUPERFOOD/INSTANT/PARENTS

Avocado is a great first food and provides good health benefits for baby. It's loaded with monounsaturated fat (the good fat), folate, potassium, and fiber. Because of the fat and high-calorie content of avocado, your baby only needs about 2 tablespoons per serving.

1 SERVING

1 ripe avocado

1. Slice avocado around the outside lengthwise.
2. Twist both sides off the seed of the avocado.
3. Scoop out 2 or 3 tablespoons of flesh from one side of the avocado.
4. Mash until desired consistency is reached.
5. Wrap remaining avocado with the seed in it with plastic wrap and store in the refrigerator or make guacamole out of the rest.

Plum Delight

BASIC/FREEZER

Picking the perfect plum is the most important part of this recipe. Choose a plum that is already ripe; it should be soft when you press it. Picking plums that are not ripe enough will result in a bitter, coarse purée.

2 OR 3 SERVINGS

1 plum

¼ cup water

1. Wash the plum thoroughly. Peel, remove the pit, and cut into quarters.
2. Place in a steaming basket over water. Cover and steam until very tender.
3. Place plum into blender.
4. Purée while gradually adding just enough water to reach a smooth consistency. Freeze extra portions for up to eight weeks.
5. If the mixture is too coarse, pass it through a fine sieve before serving and storing.

Amazing Apricot Purée

BASIC/FREEZER/INSTANT

Dried apricots will also work for this recipe. However, fresh is the best. Simmer dried apricots on the stove in a pot of water for about 8–10 minutes until tender and then purée.

3 SERVINGS

4 medium apricots, pitted

1–2 tablespoons water

1. Cut apricots in half lengthwise and combine in a blender with water.

2. Purée while gradually adding just enough water to reach a smooth consistency.

3. Work the pulp through a strong strainer to remove any fibrous materials.

4. Freeze fresh apricot purée for up to eight weeks.

Mango Tango

BASIC/FREEZER/INSTANT/PARENTS

Mangoes are the sweetest in the summer. However, unsweetened frozen mango slices will work just as well. Just thaw and purée according to these directions.

8 SERVINGS

2 medium ripe mangoes, peeled

1–2 tablespoons water

1. Remove flesh from mango.

2. Add mango to blender.

3. Purée while gradually adding just enough water to reach a smooth consistency. Freeze extra portions for up to eight weeks.

Just Peachy Purée

If peaches are not in season, buy frozen unsweetened peaches, thaw, and use to purée for your baby. Purchasing frozen fruit and vegetables is a great way to get produce out of season.

4–6 SERVINGS

4 medium peaches, skinned, pitted, and chopped

2–4 tablespoons water

1. Put peaches in a medium saucepan and cook over medium-low heat for 5–7 minutes or until soft.
2. Transfer peaches to blender.
3. Purée while gradually adding just enough water to reach a smooth consistency. Freeze extra portions for up to eight weeks.

Split Pea Purée

Split peas are a great source of protein, fiber, and iron. Combine this purée with mashed potatoes and add a dab of butter for a more savory meal. While you're already prepping those peas, why not make split pea soup for lunch?

2–4 SERVINGS

½ cup green split peas, picked and rinsed

1 cup water

1. Combine split peas and the water in a small saucepan. Bring to a boil.
2. Reduce heat, cover, and simmer for 30–45 minutes. Reserve liquid.
3. Transfer peas to a blender and purée until smooth. Add reserved liquid if necessary.

Pumpkin Patch Purée

BASIC

Canned pumpkin is available all year round and is quick and easy to make—just open the can and serve. Thin with breast milk for a nutritional boost. Make sure to buy plain pumpkin with no added spices, sugars, or dairy products.

4 SERVINGS

½ can pure pumpkin (approximately 8 ounces)

Breast milk or water for thinning as needed

1. Warm pumpkin in a small saucepan on the stovetop or in a glass dish in the microwave. Remove.

2. Add breast milk or water to thin if desired. Refrigerate remaining portions for up to three days.

One-Carrot Gold Purée

BASIC/FREEZER

Some vegetables, including carrots, may leak nitrates into the cooking water as they're boiled. For this reason, only make this purée for your baby if she is at least seven months old. As an extra precaution, do not use the cooking water when thinning out this purée; use cooled boiled water instead.

3 SERVINGS

1 cup fresh carrots (2 medium-sized carrots)

¼ cup water

1. Wash and peel the carrots. Cut into small pieces.

2. Place into a saucepan with enough water to cover the carrots. Bring the water to a boil; then simmer until the carrots are very tender, 15–20 minutes.

3. Drain the carrots and place into a blender or food processor. Purée for about 30 seconds.

4. Gradually add in freshly cooled, boiled water. Continue puréeing until smooth.

Simply Cauliflower

BASIC/FREEZER/PARENTS

Cauliflower resembles mashed potatoes when puréed in both looks and taste. However, it doesn't have all the starch. You can cook cauliflower for the family and just scoop out an unseasoned portion for baby.

3 SERVINGS

1 cup cauliflower

2 cups water

1. Wash the cauliflower thoroughly. Discard the stem and leaves and chop the florets into small pieces.

2. Put into a steamer basket. Bring to a boil and steam until tender, about 20 minutes.

3. Place into a food processor or blender, and purée for 30 seconds. Add liquid as necessary to achieve desired consistency.

Sparkling Pear Purée

BASIC/FREEZER

Pears are very sweet and make a runny consistency when puréed. Pears contain soluble fiber, which aids in digestion and can help relieve constipation. Boost the nutrition on this recipe by thickening with rice cereal.

6–8 SERVINGS

4 medium ripe pears, peeled, cored, and chopped

1. Add chopped pears to a medium-sized saucepan.

2. Cover and cook on medium-low heat for about 7 minutes, until tender. Stir frequently.

3. Transfer the cooked pears to a blender.

4. Purée to a smooth consistency. Freeze extra portions for up to eight weeks.

Green Bean Bliss

Unless you are building an emergency stash, stay away from canned beans, because they lose nutritional value in the canning process. Stick to fresh or frozen green beans for the best nutrition.

4 SERVINGS

1 cup fresh or frozen green beans, trimmed and cut

1 cup water

1. Put beans into a steamer basket, or place in a saucepan covered by an inch of water. Cover.

2. Heat to a boil; then turn down heat slightly. Steam until tender, about 5–7 minutes.

3. Place the beans into a blender. Purée to a smooth consistency by gradually adding the leftover water from steaming.

Baked Winter Squash

Butternut and acorn squash can be purchased year round, but the best prices on these are in the fall. Use them to decorate your kitchen or dining table before you are ready to cook them.

8 SERVINGS

1 butternut or acorn squash

1 cup cooled, boiled water

1. Cut squash in half and scoop out seeds.

2. Bake skin side down on a baking sheet at 350°F for 30 minutes or until flesh is tender.

3. Scoop out soft, cooked flesh and transfer to blender.

4. Purée while gradually adding just enough water to reach a smooth consistency.

Plumtastic Purée

When you have more purées in your freezer than you know what to do with, combine them with yogurt! Yogurt adds a boost of super nutrition with its probiotic qualities. Use a low-fat yogurt and have a plumtastic snack for yourself!

8 SERVINGS

3 large plums

1 cup organic whole-fat vanilla yogurt

1. Peel plums by scoring a cross on the bottom of each fruit.
2. Submerge them into boiling water for about 1 minute.
3. Peel, cut, and discard the pit. Chop plum into small pieces.
4. Steam the plum pieces for a few minutes until soft. If the plums are very ripe and soft, you will not need to steam. Purée in a blender.
5. Combine the plum purée with the vanilla yogurt and serve.
6. Store the remaining portions in the refrigerator for up to four days.

Cucumber-Melon Mashup

Cucumber and melon not only smell great together, but they taste great together. This is an instant purée because you do not need to cook the melon or cucumber. There is a little preparation, but once the seeds and skins are removed, it's smooth sailing afterwards. You may also combine this with vanilla yogurt or rice cereal to thicken.

8 SERVINGS

½ melon, peeled, seeded, and chopped

½ cucumber, peeled, seeded and chopped

4 tablespoons full-fat vanilla yogurt or baby rice cereal

1. Purée the melon and cucumber together.
2. Stir in rice cereal or yogurt to thicken.
3. Serve immediately or freeze for up to eight weeks (do not freeze with yogurt or cereal).

Nectarine King

BASIC/FREEZER

Check out your local farmers' market in the summer and stock up on nectarines for this sweet purée. Nectarines are rich in beta-carotene, potassium, and niacin.

10 SERVINGS

5 medium nectarines (washed, peeled, pitted, and halved)

Baby rice cereal

1. Steam nectarines over boiling water in a steamer basket for 2–3 minutes. Drain.

2. Purée to a smooth consistency. To thicken, add rice cereal. Freeze remaining portions for up to 8 weeks.

What's the Difference Between a Peach and a Nectarine?
Both of these are stone fruits, but the major difference is that a peach is larger and has a fuzzy outer skin, while nectarines are usually smaller, smooth on the outside, and sweeter.

Fall Pumpkin Yogurt

SUPERFOOD/INSTANT/PARENTS

When the trees are starting to change colors and fall is settling in, make this delicious recipe to celebrate the new season.

8 SERVINGS

½ cup canned organic pumpkin or fresh pumpkin purée

½ cup full-fat organic vanilla yogurt

Combine all ingredients and serve.

Cucumber Cooler

BASIC/FREEZER/INSTANT

Cucumber has a mild yet interesting taste that babies enjoy. Make big batches of this purée to freeze because it can be mixed later on with yogurt, fruit, and other vegetable purées.

4 SERVINGS

1 cucumber, peeled, seeded, and chopped

Baby rice cereal

1. Purée the cucumber to a smooth consistency.

2. Serve immediately or freeze for up to eight weeks (do not freeze with cereal). Stir in rice cereal to thicken.

Purple Beauty Eggplant Purée

BASIC/FREEZER/PARENTS

Eggplant is an excellent source of fiber and contains cancer-preventing antioxidants. Eggplant comes in many purple varieties. You can choose any kind for this recipe.

10–12 SERVINGS

1 eggplant, peeled and chopped

1. Add eggplant to a large pot. Cover with water. Bring to a boil.

2. Simmer until tender, about 10–12 minutes. Remove from heat.

3. Add eggplant to blender. Purée while gradually adding just enough water to achieve a smooth consistency.

4. Freeze remaining portions.

Zealous Zucchini

BASIC/FREEZER

Zucchini can easily be grown in your backyard. One plant can provide enough zucchini to feed your baby for many months! It is not necessary to remove the skin of the zucchini; however, you may do so if you choose. Zucchini is great with rice cereal or mashed potatoes.

2 SERVINGS

1 cup zucchini, trimmed and sliced

1. Steam for 10 minutes or until tender.
2. Purée until smooth.

Simply Broccoli

BASIC/FREEZER/SUPERFOOD

Broccoli is a terrific food for babies because it is packed with vitamin C, potassium, and folate. Try serving broccoli and cauliflower together for an even tastier meal.

3 SERVINGS

1 cup broccoli

2 cups water

1. Wash the broccoli. Chop off the stems and leaves and cut the florets into small pieces.
2. Put into a steamer basket. Bring to a boil and steam until tender, about 15 minutes.
3. Place into blender, and purée for about 30 seconds. Add water as necessary to achieve a smooth consistency.

Hiya Papaya

BASIC/FREEZER/INSTANT

Although papaya turns out okay frozen in chunks, papaya purée may become watery when frozen. Therefore, make fresh papaya purée and refrigerate for up to three or four days.

3 SERVINGS
. . . .

½ medium papaya

1–2 tablespoons breast milk or formula

1. Cut papaya in half lengthwise; scrape out the seeds and discard them.

2. Scoop out the flesh of ½ the papaya and put in a medium bowl.

3. Add breast milk or organic formula to papaya and mash with fork until smooth.

Dried Prune-a-Plenty

BASIC/INSTANT

Prunes are an amazing source of fiber, providing 2 grams of fiber per ounce. Adding prunes to your baby's diet will help her maintain a healthy gastrointestinal tract and regular bowel movements. Baby constipated? Give him prunes!

3 SERVINGS
. . . .

⅔ cup (4 ounces) pitted dried prunes

3 tablespoons water

1. Combine prunes and water in a blender.

2. Purée until smooth. Add more water to thin if necessary.

3. If the mixture is still too coarse, pass it through a fine strainer.

Crazy about Cantaloupe

BASIC/FREEZER/INSTANT/PARENTS

Sweet cantaloupe is extremely tasty and refreshing during the spring and summer months. It does not need to be cooked, making it easy to purée some for baby while you're cutting a wedge of it for yourself. Its runny consistency makes it good as a first food and is great when mixed with rice cereal.

6–8 SERVINGS

2 cups chopped cantaloupe

Purée chopped cantaloupe in a blender until smooth. Serve.

Variation for Parents: Cantaloupe Peach Cooler
Blend 2 cups chopped cantaloupe, 1 cup fresh or frozen peaches, and the juice of one freshly squeezed lemon. Add sugar to taste if desired. Garnish with a few slices of fresh peach and enjoy!

Savory Chickpea Smash

BASIC/INSTANT

Canned chickpeas, with no salt added, make this a very quick and easy purée. Keep a few cans on hand for mixing with other purées to make hummus or to keep in your emergency stash.

2 OR 3 SERVINGS

½ cup canned chickpeas

3 tablespoons water or organic chicken stock

1. Rinse and drain the chickpeas. Remove any stray hulls.
2. Place into blender, and purée for about 30 seconds.
3. Add water or stock, 1 tablespoon at a time. Continue puréeing until the mixture is smooth.

Banana Blueberry Buckle

Experts say to eat a handful of blueberries a day for good health. While you're making this for baby, make a banana blueberry buckle smoothie with 100 percent grape juice for a powerful antioxidant boost for yourself!

2 SERVINGS

2 tablespoons fresh blueberries

½ large ripe banana

Purée blueberries and banana in a blender. Serve immediately.

Superfood Duo

Blueberries are packed with more powerful antioxidants than any other fruit, and bananas are an amazing source for potassium. Serve your baby this purée once per day for excellent health.

Pumpkin-Parsnip Purée

Parsnips may be hard to find in some local grocery stores. Try looking for parsnips at the farmers' market or other markets that specialize in fresh produce.

2 SERVINGS

1 small parsnip

4 tablespoons pure canned pumpkin

1. Peel parsnip and cut into small slices or chunks.
2. Steam parsnip using either a steamer basket or microwave.
3. Purée parsnip using reserved steaming water to achieve age-appropriate consistency.
4. Combine parsnip purée and pumpkin purée.

Pumpkin-Pear-Rice Medley

SUPERFOOD

Whether you choose Bartlett, D'Anjou, or Bosc pears for this recipe, your baby will go gaga for the goodness of this recipe.

2 SERVINGS

4 tablespoons prepared iron-fortified rice cereal (with either breast milk or formula)

2 tablespoons Pumpkin Patch Purée (Chapter 4) or pure canned pumpkin

2 tablespoons Sparkling Pear Purée (Chapter 4)

Combine all ingredients.

Green Beans and Rice Combo

FREEZER/SUPERFOOD

Use your frozen Green Bean Bliss cubes to combine with the rice cereal for this recipe. Out of frozen purée? Steam more beans, purée, and freeze!

1 SERVING

2 tablespoons prepared iron-fortified rice cereal (with either breast milk or formula)

2 tablespoons Green Bean Bliss (Chapter 4)

Combine all ingredients.

Mango, Green Bean, and Rice Mélange

FREEZER/SUPERFOOD

Although to adults this combination might seem unappealing, stretch your baby's horizons by combining different food tastes and textures. Remember the nutritional benefits when combining foods.

1 SERVING

2 tablespoons prepared iron-fortified rice cereal (with either breast milk or formula)

2 tablespoons Green Bean Bliss (Chapter 4)

2 tablespoons Mango Tango (Chapter 4)

Combine all ingredients.

Peachy Mango Rice Cereal

FREEZER/SUPERFOOD

These two fruits complement each other with organic sweetness.

1 SERVING

4 tablespoons prepared iron-fortified rice cereal (with either breast milk or formula)

2 tablespoons Mango Tango (Chapter 4)

2 tablespoons Just Peachy Purée (Chapter 4)

Combine all ingredients.

Freezing the Basics
Make large portions of the single-ingredient purées in the beginning of this chapter and save preparation time. Mix and match cubes to make a complete meal.

Sweet Peas (Made Sweeter with) Banana Rice Cereal

SUPERFOOD

If your little sweetie doesn't love sweet peas, this combination might do the trick.

1 SERVING

2 tablespoons prepared iron-fortified
rice cereal (with either breast milk or
formula)

2 tablespoons mashed banana

2 tablespoons Pretty Peas (Chapter 4)

Combine all ingredients.

Banana Oatmeal Mash

SUPERFOOD/INSTANT

Bananas pair very well with oatmeal cereal. This is sure to be a popular hit with your baby. Remember that bananas tend to constipate, so make sure you offer meals with apples, pears, or prunes to help prevent it.

1 SERVING

2 tablespoons prepared iron-fortified
oatmeal cereal (with either breast milk
or formula)

2 tablespoons mashed banana

Combine all ingredients.

Papaya-Pear Oatmeal

SUPERFOOD

Yum . . . the goodness of oatmeal. This fruity, delicious oatmeal is healthy for baby with a unique combination you won't find on the shelf—only in your kitchen.

2 SERVINGS

4 tablespoons prepared iron-fortified oatmeal cereal (with either breast milk or formula)

2 tablespoons Hiya Papaya (Chapter 4)

2 tablespoons Sparkling Pear Purée (Chapter 4)

Combine all ingredients.

Banana-Apricot Oatmeal

SUPERFOOD/INSTANT

This combination includes lots of nutrients that a growing baby needs, including potassium, iron, and vitamin A. Make sure the apricots are nice and sweet, just like your baby.

2 SERVINGS

4 tablespoons prepared iron-fortified oatmeal cereal (with either breast milk or formula)

2 tablespoons mashed banana

2 tablespoons Amazing Apricot Purée (Chapter 4)

Combine all ingredients.

Apple-tastic Oatmeal

SUPERFOOD

Serving apple oatmeal is a great way for your baby to start her day. The rich flavors of the apple are sure to wake up your baby's senses so that she can smile all day!

1 SERVING

2 tablespoons prepared iron-fortified oatmeal cereal (with either breast milk or formula)
2 tablespoons Enchanting Apple (Chapter 4)

Combine all ingredients.

Get Your Apples Local!
Apples are grown all throughout the United States, and many neighborhoods have apples growing on trees in their backyards. Befriend your neighbors for some fresh organic apples or support your local farms and go and pick your own!

Apple-Papaya Porridge

SUPERFOOD

This combination is a sweet and yummy way to start the day (and you know the old saying about an apple a day . . . !).

2 SERVINGS

4 tablespoons prepared iron-fortified oatmeal cereal (with either breast milk or formula)
2 tablespoons Hiya Papaya (Chapter 4)
2 tablespoons Enchanting Apple (Chapter 4)

Combine all ingredients.

Peachy Pumpkin Oatmeal

SUPERFOOD

The combination of pumpkin and peach will result in a vibrant orange color and subtly sweet flavor no child can resist. But what's better is that you're serving your baby a meal packed with lots of iron and fiber. It's a win-win!

2 SERVINGS

4 tablespoons prepared iron-fortified oatmeal cereal (with either breast milk or formula)

2 tablespoons Pumpkin Patch Purée (Chapter 4) or 100 percent canned pumpkin

2 tablespoons Just Peachy Purée (Chapter 4)

Combine all ingredients.

Creamy Avocado Barley Cereal

SUPERFOOD/INSTANT

Avocados will turn brown after sitting out for a while, so serve this purée immediately after preparation.

1 SERVING

2 tablespoons prepared iron-fortified barley cereal (with either breast milk or formula)

2 tablespoons freshly mashed avocado

Combine all ingredients.

Avocado Facts
Avocados were introduced to the United States from Mexico in the nineteenth century. Ninety-five percent of avocado production is cultivated in California.

Prune-Barley Bowel Helper

SUPERFOOD/INSTANT

This is a great recipe to use if your baby feels constipated. The high fiber content in barley and prunes can help move things along.

1 SERVING

2 tablespoons prepared iron-fortified barley cereal (with either breast milk or formula)

2 tablespoons Dried Prune-a-Plenty (Chapter 4)

Combine all ingredients.

Apple-Plum-Barley Cereal

FREEZER/SUPERFOOD

This is a great way to use apples or plums that are ever so slightly past their prime and no longer ideal for eating whole. You can also freeze this superfood purée, so why not make a big batch?

2 SERVINGS

4 tablespoons prepared iron-fortified barley cereal (with either breast milk or formula)

2 tablespoons Enchanting Apple (Chapter 4)

2 tablespoons Plumtastic Purée (Chapter 4)

Combine all ingredients.

Avocado-Banana Mash

Keep fresh banana and avocado in your baby's lunch bag to make an instant purée while on the run. They both come in their own convenient packaging!

1 SERVING

2 tablespoons freshly mashed avocado

2 tablespoons mashed banana

Combine all ingredients and mash with a fork until desired consistency.

Ripen Those Bananas

If your bananas are a little green when you purchase them, place them in a brown bag and allow them to ripen undisturbed. Check the next day to discover your bananas have ripened!

Avocado-Pumpkin Mash

When making this recipe, swirl the pumpkin purée into the mashed avocado with a knife. Serve it in a glass bowl for a dazzling presentation.

1 SERVING

2 tablespoons mashed avocado

2 tablespoons canned pumpkin or Pumpkin Patch Purée (Chapter 4)

Combine all ingredients.

Apricot-Pear Purée

If your baby is having trouble with bowel movements, this is a great purée to turn to—pears are filled with fiber and can be used to help alleviate constipation.

1 SERVING
. . . .
2 tablespoons Amazing Apricot Purée
(Chapter 4)
**2 tablespoons Sparkling Pear
Purée** (Chapter 4)

Combine all ingredients.

Mango-Pear Purée

FREEZER

Give your baby a tiny taste of the tropics with this purée, which features mango paired with pear (for extra fiber)! Make a bunch in advance and freeze for a ray of sunshine on a rainy day.

1 SERVING
. . . .
2 tablespoons Mango Tango
(Chapter 4)
**2 tablespoons Sparkling Pear
Purée** (Chapter 4)

Combine all ingredients.

Mango-Banana Mashup

FREEZER/SUPERFOOD/INSTANT/PARENTS

While you're making this purée for baby, reserve the remaining fruit for a Fruity Flakes breakfast for yourself.

1 SERVING

½ mashed banana

¼ ripe mango, peeled and seeded

Combine all ingredients.

Variation for Parents: Fruity Flakes
Cut bananas and mangoes into small chunks. Add on top of your favorite cereal, such as Corn Flakes, or flakes with oats. The freshness of the fruit combined with the cereal will perk you up in the morning!

Papaya and Banana Blend

SUPERFOOD/INSTANT

If papayas are not in season, add a splash of 100 percent (no sugar added) papaya juice to the banana and your baby will still reap the nutritional benefits. You can store the remaining banana portion in the refrigerator for a couple of days. The peel will turn brown, but the banana flesh will stay yellow and fresh.

1 SERVING

2 tablespoons Hiya Papaya
(Chapter 4)

2 tablespoons mashed banana

Combine all ingredients.

Mouthwatering Peach-Avocado Mash

SUPERFOOD

Here's a wonderful purée to make when summer peaches are in season! For an unforgettable experience, visit a pick-your-own farm and pluck your very own fresh, organic peaches off the tree.

1 SERVING
....
2 tablespoons Just Peachy Purée (Chapter 4)

2 tablespoons mashed avocado

Combine all ingredients and mash with a fork until smooth.

Are Unusual Combinations Tasty for Baby?
Because babies are developing taste buds, it's okay to try unconventional combinations of fruits and vegetables, even if they don't seem like they would taste good together. Your child may love an offbeat mixture of plums and sweet peas. Experimenting will be fun, and you may learn a thing or two about new food combos your baby actually enjoys.

Plum-Pear Yogurt Yum-Yum

SUPERFOOD

Dried plums can also be used in place of fresh plums.

3 SERVINGS
....
2 tablespoons Plumtastic Purée (Chapter 4)

2 tablespoons Sparkling Pear Purée (Chapter 4)

2 tablespoons full-fat organic vanilla yogurt

1. Combine all ingredients.

2. Remaining portions will keep in the refrigerator for up to four days.

Just Peachy Sparkler

Ignite your baby's senses with this refreshing combination. The peaches and pears can be puréed raw once your baby is an established purée connoisseur.

1 SERVING
....

2 tablespoons Just Peachy Purée (Chapter 4)

2 tablespoons Sparkling Pear Purée (Chapter 4)

Combine all ingredients.

Peachy Rice Purée

When peaches are in season, there's nothing more decadent. This sweet, smooth cereal gives your baby a taste of the delicious foods she'll enjoy as she grows up eating your wholesome meals.

1 SERVING
....

2 tablespoons prepared iron-fortified rice cereal (with either breast milk or formula)

2 tablespoons Just Peachy Purée (Chapter 4)

Combine prepared rice cereal and peach purée.

Baby's Gone Bananas for Pumpkin

SUPERFOOD

Use this flavorful purée as a spread on toast or teething biscuits when teething starts at around eight or nine months.

1 SERVING

2 tablespoons mashed banana

2 tablespoons Pumpkin Patch Purée (Chapter 4)

Combine all ingredients.

Blissful Greens

SUPERFOOD

This delicious combo is especially healthy for baby, providing a nice dose of healthy fat, vitamin K, vitamin C, potassium, and iron.

1 SERVING

2 tablespoons Green Bean Bliss (Chapter 4)

2 tablespoons mashed avocado

Combine all ingredients.

Sweet Pea Tango

Mangoes and sweet peas tango in perfect harmony in this purée. When you find mangoes on sale, buy a bunch and make batches to freeze!

1 SERVING
. . . .
2 tablespoons Pretty Peas (Chapter 4)
2 tablespoons Mango Tango (Chapter 4)

Combine all ingredients.

Bright Zucchini and Rice

Zucchini squash comes in vibrant hues of green and yellow. Experiment with different colors for a colorful meal your baby will enjoy.

1 SERVING
. . . .
1 medium zucchini
2 tablespoons prepared iron-fortified rice cereal (with either breast milk or formula)

1. Cut off ends of zucchini; do not peel.

2. Cut into slices and steam zucchini squash pieces for 4–6 minutes to soften. Reserve water.

3. Purée the zucchini while adding enough water to reach a smooth consistency.

4. Combine 2 tablespoons zucchini purée with 2 tablespoons prepared iron-fortified cereal and serve. Freeze remaining zucchini purée for up to eight weeks.

Carrot-Apple Gold Purée

Both carrots and apples stem from the earth's richness. This purée is as good as gold.

2 SERVINGS
....

1 carrot, peeled and cut into chunks

½ cup Homemade Applesauce

1. Steam carrot using either a steamer basket or microwave until soft and tender.

2. Purée carrot using reserved steaming water to achieve age-appropriate consistency.

3. Combine carrot and applesauce.

Homemade Applesauce

No need to buy store-bought applesauce when you can make your own, with apples fresh from the farm! Apples provide a wealth of vitamin C for immunity.

12–14 SERVINGS
....

12 Gala apples, peeled, cored, and cubed

¼ teaspoon cinnamon

Dash of pure vanilla extract

Enough water to cover apples

1. Combine apple chunks, cinnamon, and vanilla in a large pot.

2. Cover apples with water.

3. Cook until apples are very tender and start to break apart.

4. Transfer apples to blender and purée for a smooth consistency or pulse on and off for a chunkier texture. Serve warm or cold.

5. Freeze remaining portions.

Apple-Pear-Barley Cereal

A good source of vitamin A, folate, and even protein, barley packs a nutritional punch! Pair with the sweet goodness of apples and pears and you've got a well-rounded meal for your little one.

1 SERVING

2 tablespoons iron-fortified barley cereal (prepared with breast milk or formula)

2 tablespoons Enchanting Apple (Chapter 4)

2 tablespoons Sparkling Pear Purée (Chapter 4)

Combine all ingredients.

Carrot–Sweet Potato Purée

This flavorful—and vibrant!—dish is nutritiously rich with antioxidants.

2 SERVINGS

1 carrot

4 tablespoons Simply Sweet Potato (Chapter 4)

1. Peel carrot and cut into small slices or chunks.

2. Steam carrot using a steamer basket.

3. Transfer carrot to a blender or food processor and purée using reserved steaming water to achieve a smooth consistency.

4. Combine carrot purée with Simply Sweet Potato purée.

Island Breakfast Cereal

SUPERFOOD/INSTANT

Bring the islands to your kitchen by using frozen fruit in winter when local options are scarce.

4 SERVINGS

4 tablespoons prepared iron-fortified barley cereal (with either breast milk or formula)

2 tablespoons Hiya Papaya (Chapter 4)

2 tablespoons Mango Tango (Chapter 4)

Combine all ingredients.

Blushing Banana and Apricot

SUPERFOOD/INSTANT

Make sure the apricots are sweet when you're ready to make this recipe. If apricots aren't in season or aren't quite ripe yet, you can substitute dried apricots.

1 SERVING

2 tablespoons Amazing Apricot Purée (Chapter 4)

2 tablespoons mashed banana

Combine all ingredients.

Prune, Apricot, and Yogurt Blend

SUPERFOOD/INSTANT

This is the perfect creamy, sweet combo to serve to your constipated little one. Prunes help move baby's bowels, and the yogurt soothes the digestive tract with all sorts of good bacteria.

3 SERVINGS

2 tablespoons full-fat Greek yogurt or plain yogurt

2 tablespoons Amazing Apricot Purée (Chapter 4)

2 tablespoons Dried Prune-a-Plenty (Chapter 4)

Combine all ingredients.

Plummy Potatoes

FREEZER

The variety of potatoes available at the market can sometimes be mind-boggling. For this recipe, note that white russet or butter gold potatoes work best because they get super smooth when puréed.

2 SERVINGS

1 small potato

⅛ cup water

1 small, ripe plum

1. Wash and peel potato and cut into small chunks.

2. Bring potato and water to a boil in a small saucepan. Cook until tender.

3. Wash the plum thoroughly. Peel, remove the pit, and cut into quarters. Steam the plum pieces for a few minutes until soft. If the plums are very ripe and soft, you will not need to steam.

4. Combine fresh plum and cooked potato in blender. Purée until smooth.

Two-Potato Dream

FREEZER/PARENTS

The two flavors of sweet and buttery collide in this wonderful duo. Instead of blending together, blend them separately and then swirl the two purées together with a butter knife for an interesting effect.

6 SERVINGS

1 small Yukon Gold potato

⅛ cup water

½ teaspoon butter (optional)

4 tablespoons Simply Sweet Potato (Chapter 4)

1. Wash and peel potato and cut into small chunks.

2. Add potatoes and water to a small saucepan. Bring to a boil and cook until tender.

3. Transfer potato to a blender. Purée.

4. Combine both potato purées. Stir in butter if desired.

Squash-Apple-Pear Medley

FREEZER/SUPERFOOD

If you aren't able to find butternut squash at your local grocery or farmers' market, feel free to use another variety of winter squash—or even pumpkin!—for this recipe.

6 SERVINGS

½ cup peeled butternut squash chunks

¼ cup water

2 tablespoons Enchanting Apple (Chapter 4)

2 tablespoons Sparkling Pear Purée (Chapter 4)

1. Combine squash and water in a medium saucepan. Bring to a boil.

2. Stir while cooking to ensure that squash cooks evenly.

3. Cook until tender, 8–10 minutes.

4. Transfer squash to a food processor or blender. Purée, using reserved cooking water as necessary to achieve age-appropriate consistency.

5. Combine squash with Enchanting Apple purée and Sparkling Pear Purée.

Butternut Squash Plus Carrot Purée

Take advantage of autumn when both of these vegetables are in season. Don't forget to freeze any leftovers to enjoy in the spring!

1 SERVING

½ cup butternut squash chunks

2 tablespoons One-Carrot Gold Purée (Chapter 4)

1. Steam large butternut squash pieces for 25 minutes to soften and loosen the skin. When cool enough to handle, remove skin from squash and cut into 2-inch cubes.

2. Add squash to blender and purée until desired consistency is reached.

3. Combine 2 tablespoons of resulting butternut squash purée with carrot purée and serve.

4. Freeze remaining butternut squash for up to eight weeks.

Apple-Banana Oatmeal

Most babies prefer the taste of sweet apples over tart apples, so it's best to stay away from Granny Smith apples when making apple purées for the earliest eaters.

3 SERVINGS

2 tablespoons prepared iron-fortified oatmeal cereal (with either breast milk or formula)

2 tablespoons Enchanting Apple (Chapter 4)

2 tablespoons mashed banana

Combine all ingredients.

MENUS FOR SIX- TO SEVEN-MONTH-OLDS

Always introduce new foods separately for four to seven consecutive days to watch for signs of allergies. Once your baby has shown no reaction to the foods alone, you can introduce mixtures of previously tolerated foods and follow the sample menu. **EVERY DAY: Breast milk or formula:** 24–32 ounces per day **Iron-fortified infant cereal:** ¼ cup per day

WEEK 1	MONDAY	TUESDAY	WEDNESDAY
	Homemade Rice Cereal	Homemade Oatmeal Cereal	Homemade Rice Cereal
	Avocado Mash	Pumpkin Patch Purée	Simply Sweet Potato
	Blushing Bananas	Just Peachy Purée	Amazing Apricot Purée
THURSDAY	FRIDAY	SATURDAY	SUNDAY
Homemade Oatmeal Cereal	Homemade Rice Cereal	Homemade Oatmeal Cereal	Homemade Rice Cereal
Green Bean Bliss	Crazy about Cantaloupe	Mango Tango	Sparkling Pear Purée
Blushing Bananas	Baked Winter Squash	Green Bean Bliss	Zealous Zucchini

WEEK 2	MONDAY	TUESDAY	WEDNESDAY
	Apple-tastic Oatmeal	Homemade Barley Cereal	Homemade Barley Cereal; Avocado Mash
	Avocado-Banana Mash	Squash-Apple-Pear Medley	Simply Sweet Potato
	Green Beans and Rice Combo	Plumtastic Purée	Peachy Mango Rice Cereal
THURSDAY	FRIDAY	SATURDAY	SUNDAY
Banana Oatmeal Mash	Island Breakfast Cereal	Papaya-Pear Oatmeal	Homemade Barley Cereal; Plum Delight
Plummy Potatoes	Simply Broccoli	Green Bean Bliss	Bright Zucchini and Rice
Hiya Papaya	Enchanting Apple	Cucumber-Melon Mashup	Plum-Pear Yogurt Yum-Yum

WEEK 3	MONDAY	TUESDAY	WEDNESDAY
	Apple-Plum-Barley Cereal	Blushing Banana and Apricot; Homemade Rice Cereal	Apple-tastic Oatmeal
	Simply Sweet Potato	Split Pea Purée	Bright Zucchini and Rice
	Pumpkin-Pear-Rice Medley	Mango Tango	Butternut Squash Plus Carrot Purée

THURSDAY	FRIDAY	SATURDAY	SUNDAY
Banana Oatmeal Mash	Island Breakfast Cereal	Peachy Mango Rice Cereal	Homemade Barley Cereal; Plum Delight
Green Bean Bliss	Sweet Peas (Made Sweeter with) Banana Rice Cereal	Baked Winter Squash	Bright Zucchini and Rice
Two-Potato Dream	Simply Cauliflower	Cucumber-Melon Mashup	Apple-Papaya Porridge

WEEK 4	MONDAY	TUESDAY	WEDNESDAY
	Homemade Rice Cereal	Homemade Barley Cereal; Avocado Mash	Apple-tastic Oatmeal
	Avocado-Banana Mash	Simply Sweet Potato	Plummy Potatoes
	Just Peachy Purée; Homemade Rice Cereal	Mango Tango	Butternut Squash Plus Carrot Purée

THURSDAY	FRIDAY	SATURDAY	SUNDAY
Banana Oatmeal Mash	Island Breakfast Cereal	Peachy Mango Rice Cereal	Homemade Barley Cereal; Plum Delight
Green Bean Bliss	Plumtastic Purée	Baked Winter Squash	Bright Zucchini and Rice
Two-Potato Dream	Simply Cauliflower	Hiya Papaya	Enchanting Apple

CHAPTER 5

MORE FLAVOR TO SAVOR (EIGHT TO NINE MONTHS)

Introducing Semismooth Purées

It's time for your little explorer to become more adventurous in trying new flavors, textures, and even spices! This chapter introduces more food combinations that include spices such as cinnamon, vanilla, and mint as well as meat purées such as chicken and beef. From eight months old, start puréeing your child's meal to a semismooth consistency to allow your baby plenty of chewing practice. You may even notice a tooth or two popping through! Milk is still a very important part of your child's diet, so make sure she is getting 24–32 ounces of breast milk or iron-fortified infant formula per day.

You may continue serving all of the meals in Chapter 4, and you will find that you will be able to mix and match those basic purées with the new flavors of spices and meat from this chapter, so keep those frozen purées! Continue serving grain cereals and about ¼–½ cup of fruits and vegetables per day. You may also introduce Biter Biscuits or Baby Biscotti once your child has developed a pincher grasp and can hold objects. Those foods tend to calm teething babies and give a good introduction to self-feeding. Other foods you can use to encourage self-feeding include rice cakes, diced bananas, and cereal Os.

Allow your baby to sit in a highchair for each feeding and at family mealtimes. Remember that many meals can be prepared along with the family's dinner, so make the family meals count and eat along with your baby.

SECOND-STAGE CUISINES: EIGHT OR NINE MONTHS

By eight months, you will begin to tell by the looks of your little butterball that your hard work in making healthy organic baby purées is paying off! Your baby has taken another step in the development ladder of feeding—way to go! Your baby can now sit alone without support and is growing rapidly. She can pick up small items with her thumb and finger. She's aced eating the yummy purées in the first stage and can now move on to a semismooth consistency. Breast milk or formula is still very important, and she should drink 24–32 ounces of breast milk or iron-fortified infant formula per day. She can continue with the grain cereals, fruit, and vegetables, and may take about ¼–½ cup of each of these per day. She can now have cheese, pasta, and mild seasonings and finally gets to experience meat purées. If her pincher grasp is ready, offer her finger foods such as soft crackers, toast, cereal Os, or teething biscuits.

The following list includes some new flavors to add to your baby's diet:

- 100 percent fruit juice (no sugar added)
- Beef
- Chicken
- Cheese
- Fish
- Finger foods (such as cereal Os and teething biscuits)
- Lamb
- Leafy greens
- Lentils
- Pasta
- Pork
- Scrambled or hard-boiled egg yolks
- Spices (pure vanilla, cinnamon, nutmeg, etc.)
- Whole-grain rice

Although you'll see grocery aisles packed with fruit juice, many of these are loaded down with excess sugars and preservatives. Make sure your baby only has between 2–4 ounces of all-natural, 100 percent fruit juice per day. Too much juice can cause a sweet tooth and cavities to develop if allowed to drink too much without brushing. Additionally, drinking excessive amounts of juice can lead to obesity problems and overfeeding. Take care to offer juice sparingly at this age. Brush your child's teeth, even if only a few are present, with fluoride-free toothpaste two to three times per day. This will teach your child important brushing habits and promote healthy teeth throughout his life. Offer your child plenty of water once the juice requirement is met.

Broccoli and Cauliflower Bathed in Cheddar

FREEZER/SUPERFOOD/PARENTS

Broccoli and cauliflower go great together in this cheesy dish. Purée baby's portion, but don't purée yours!

4–6 SERVINGS

1½ cups broccoli florets, chopped

¾ cup cauliflower, chopped

CHEESE SAUCE

1 tablespoon unsalted butter

1 tablespoon all-purpose flour

1 cup half-and-half (or whole milk)

5 tablespoons grated mild Cheddar cheese

1. Steam broccoli and cauliflower in steamer basket until fork tender.

2. Meanwhile, melt the unsalted butter in a saucepan over medium-low heat. Stir in flour to form a paste.

3. Gradually stir in the milk and bring to a boil. Simmer over low heat until thickened.

4. Stir in grated cheese until melted. Remove from heat.

5. Add the cooked broccoli and cauliflower to blender and purée to a semismooth consistency. Remove from blender.

6. Spoon in cheese sauce as needed. Freeze remaining portions for up to eight weeks.

Use the Cross Blade

Some blenders come with a cross blade and a flat blade. The cross blade is used for puréeing, chopping, blending, mixing, and grating. The straight, flat blade is used for grinding and chopping foods harder or coarser in texture such as dried fruit, nuts, or coffee beans. Use the cross blade for making purées.

Fruity Chicken Stew

This fruitylicious meal combines a serving of protein, fruit, vegetables, and whole grain, all in one meal!

5 SERVINGS

1 small boneless skinless chicken breast (about 4 ounces)

2 cups water

1 medium carrot

½ medium apple

½ very ripe peach

½ cup cooked brown rice

Water or breast milk for thinning as needed

1. Wash the chicken thoroughly, cut into 1-inch pieces, and place in a saucepan. Cover with water and bring to a boil, and cook for about 10 minutes.

2. Wash, peel, and slice the carrot into ½-inch chunks. Add to the cooking pot.

3. Wash, peel, and chop the apple into ½-inch cubes. Add to the cooking pot, and continue cooking until everything is completely cooked and tender, about 20–25 minutes longer.

4. Wash the peach and remove the pit and skin. Dice.

5. Once cooled, place the stewed ingredients into a food processor, along with the cooked rice and diced peach. Purée until smooth, adding water or breast milk to thin it out.

White or Brown Rice?

Although brown rice is healthier because it contains good complex carbohydrates that provide sustained energy, you can also use white rice instead of brown rice in any of these recipes.

Cheesy Mashed Potatoes

Serve this recipe alone or add it with a meat purée such as lamb, chicken, or beef.

8–12 SERVINGS

2 cups water

4 baking potatoes, peeled and chopped

4 tablespoons grated Parmesan cheese

Pat of unsalted butter

1. Add water and potatoes to a medium pot. Bring to a boil.

2. Simmer over medium heat for about 10 minutes or until tender, stirring occasionally.

3. Remove potatoes with a slotted spoon and mash with a potato masher or fork. Add more water and mash until the potatoes are a smooth consistency, or purée in a blender.

4. Remove potatoes and add Parmesan cheese and unsalted butter. Blend well.

5. Serve warm. Freeze remaining portions.

Soak the Starch Away

Yukon Gold and russet potatoes are high in starch, a white, tasteless carbohydrate found in potatoes and other foods. Peel and cut potatoes and submerge in cold water for up to 4 hours to remove some of the starch. Boiling potatoes also helps remove starch.

Puréed Collard Greens

Although collards and other leafy greens contain nitrates, by eight months old your baby can safely have these leafy greens. Spinach and kale are great substitutes for the collards in this recipe. Add texture to this purée by adding crumbles of soft cornbread.

4 SERVINGS

4 cups collards, washed and trimmed

2 cups chicken broth or water

2 tablespoons chopped onion

1 garlic clove, pressed

1 tablespoon extra-virgin olive oil

1. Add collards, broth, onion, and garlic to a medium pot.

2. Boil in broth or water for about 15 minutes, or until the vegetables turn a bright green color.

3. Allow greens to cool; then transfer to blender with a slotted spoon. Add olive oil.

4. Purée while gradually adding water until smooth.

What Makes Fruit and Vegetables Green?
Chlorophyll, a natural plant pigment, gives foods such as collard greens, kiwi, broccoli, and peas a green color. Dark, leafy greens and other dark green beauties also contain the antioxidant lutein, which helps protect eyes from damage.

Chicken and Barley Stew

Stews turn out nice and tender when set to cook low and slow. If you want to save energy, throw everything into your slow cooker, set to low, and dinner will be ready 8–10 hours later.

5 SERVINGS

1 small chicken breast (about 4 ounces)

1 medium carrot

1 small white potato

¼ cup cooked barley

1 cup water

Water or breast milk for thinning as needed

1. Wash the chicken thoroughly and cut into 1-inch pieces. Place in a saucepan. Cover with water and bring to a boil, and cook for about 10 minutes.

2. Wash, peel, and slice the carrot into ½-inch chunks. Add to the cooking pot.

3. Wash, peel, and chop the potato into ½-inch cubes. Add to the cooking pot, and continue cooking until everything is completely cooked and tender, about 20–25 minutes longer.

4. Once cooled, place the stewed ingredients into a food processor, along with the cooked barley.

5. Purée until smooth, adding water or breast milk as needed to thin.

Keep the Tooth Fairy Happy

From the time that first tooth starts to pop through, it's important to maintain your child's teeth and gums. Dilute all juices for baby with water and avoid adding sugar to meals. Sugar contributes to tooth decay, even the natural sugars found in food. Use a fluoride-free toothpaste to brush your child's teeth and gums at least twice per day.

Pear Oatmeal

Ever heard of pear oatmeal? That's the beauty of making your own purées. You can make oatmeal and many other dishes in combinations that you won't find at the store.

2 SERVINGS
. . . .

1 cup water

¼ cup regular oats (not quick-cooking)

½ **very ripe pear**

1. Grind the oats into a powder using either a food processor or blender. Alternatively, a mortar and pestle makes a terrific grinder for a small amount.

2. Pour the water into a small saucepan. Bring to a rolling boil. Add the powdered oats to the boiling water, stirring constantly for about 30 seconds.

3. Cover the pot, turn down the heat to low, and simmer for 8–10 minutes, or until the oats are smooth and thick. Stir occasionally to prevent sticking and burning.

4. Remove the core and skin from the pear. Dice into pieces, and then fork-mash on a plate until completely smooth.

5. Mix the pear with the cooled cereal.

Don't Skip Out on Snacks
Even if you feed your baby a hearty meal, such as oatmeal or a hearty stew, that won't be enough to tide him over until lunch. Babies need to eat every couple of hours no matter what. Actually, eating small portions, every 2 or 3 hours is healthier for everyone for sustained energy and body metabolism.

Baby-Style Beef Stew

This is a meal everyone in the family can enjoy. Just ramp up the recipe accordingly and scoop out enough to purée for baby. Add salt and pepper and any other seasonings you like to the family portion.

4 SERVINGS

¼ cup white flour

6 cups water, divided

2 cups chopped stewed beef or beef roast

1 carrot, peeled and sliced

½ medium-sized russet potato, peeled and diced

¼ cup chopped celery

¼ cup chopped yellow onion

1 garlic clove, pressed

1 bay leaf

1. Whisk flour and 1 cup warm water together in a separate bowl until dissolved. Set aside.

2. Combine all ingredients, including flour/water mixture, in a large pot.

3. Bring to a boil.

4. Reduce heat to a low setting and simmer for 90 minutes or until all ingredients are falling apart.

5. Remove from heat and cool slightly.

6. Transfer ingredients to a blender or food processor and purée until desired consistency is reached. If the consistency is too chunky, gradually add water and purée to thin the mixture.

Slow and Low

Use your slow cooker for making stews and one-pot meals. Slow cookers make meat incredibly tender, making puréeing or fork mashing a breeze. Add all the ingredients to the slow cooker in the morning before you go to work. By the time you get home, it will be ready and waiting for you.

Popeye's Spinach Meal

If the flavor of spinach seems too strong for baby, adding it with the potatoes will make it more acceptable.

6 SERVINGS

1 medium-sized baking potato

½ small onion (optional)

Unsalted butter (optional)

½ cup water

1 cup fresh or frozen spinach

1. Wash, peel, and chop potato into small chunks.

2. Peel and slice the onion into thin pieces. Sauté in a deep nonstick pan until soft and translucent. If the onion sticks, use some unsalted butter in the pan. Avoid using cooking oil.

3. Add the diced potato and water to the pan. Bring to a boil; then turn down the heat and simmer until the potato is tender, about 25–30 minutes. Add more water if the potato sticks to the pan.

4. If using fresh spinach, wash the leaves thoroughly, chop, and remove all stems. Boil in a pan of shallow water for about 10 minutes. If using frozen spinach, defrost and cook according to the package directions.

5. Combine the cooked potatoes, onion, and spinach in a blender.

6. Purée until smooth, adding as much water as necessary for age-appropriate consistency.

Give Your Greens a Bath

Get rid of all the dirt and sand found in fresh leafy greens like spinach, collards, and kale by making a bath for it in your kitchen sink. Submerge the greens in a large bowl of water and allow it to soak for a few minutes. Drain. Repeat the process until the water is clear.

Wholesome Chicken, Carrot, and Rice Dinner

How often do you prepare chicken, carrots, and rice for dinner? Prepare this family classic using your favorite spices, but reserve unseasoned portions for baby.

4 SERVINGS

1 medium carrot

¼ cup cooked brown rice

½ cup cooked chicken

1. Wash and peel the carrots. Cut into small pieces.

2. Place in a saucepan with enough water to cover the carrots. Bring the water to a boil; then simmer until the carrots are very tender, about 15–20 minutes.

3. Place the carrots in a food processor or blender with the rice.

4. Dice chicken and add to the food processor.

5. Purée while gradually adding water to reach a semi-smooth consistency.

Using Stocks and Broth

Instead of using plain water to prepare foods and purées, consider adding chicken or vegetable stock or broth to add flavor to liven up second-stage purées and to thin them. Make your own or purchase low-sodium organic stock from the store. However, stay clear of the square bouillon cubes, which contain a tremendous amount of salt not suitable for babies.

Apple Date Purée

Soft and plump dates make this purée a lot easier to process. This recipe requires a few hours of presoaking, so while you're waiting on them, make applesauce out of the remaining apples you have on hand.

3 SERVINGS

¼ cup fresh dates

1 medium apple

Water or breast milk for thinning as needed

1. Remove the pits from the dates. Cover with water in a dish, and allow to soak for 3–4 hours, or until they are completely hydrated.

2. Peel and core the apple. Cut into pieces and put into a saucepan.

3. Cover the apple with water; then bring to a boil. Simmer for 25 minutes or until completely tender.

4. Drain the apple pieces and combine with soaked dates in a food processor or blender. Purée until mixture is smooth, adding water or breast milk as necessary.

Natural Baby Laxatives

Dates, plums, prunes, and figs are among many foods that provide excellent relief for constipation, especially in babies. Just like adults, babies need relief of occasional constipation. Offering these foods in the form of purées should do the job!

Garden Veg and Lentil Dinner

FREEZER/SUPERFOOD/PARENTS

Lentils feature prominently in cuisines from around the world, including the Middle East and India. For you, serve as a soup by adding spices and more broth if desired.

4–6 SERVINGS

2 tablespoons carrots, peeled and chopped

2 tablespoons celery, chopped

2 tablespoons sweet onions, chopped

1 tablespoon extra-virgin olive oil

2 cups chicken or vegetable stock

½ cup brown lentils, picked and rinsed

2 tablespoons tomatoes, seeded and chopped

1. Sauté carrots, celery, and sweet onions in extra-virgin olive oil in a medium pot until onions are translucent.

2. Add stock, lentils, and tomatoes and bring to a boil over medium-high heat.

3. Reduce heat to low and simmer gently with lid tilted for 30–45 minutes, or until lentils are tender.

4. Purée to the desired consistency and serve. Freeze remaining portions up to eight weeks.

Love Lentils

Lentils are rich in iron and promote healthy brain development. These heart-healthy legumes are sold in green, red, or brown colors, whole or split. Store dried lentils in an airtight container in your pantry for up to twelve months.

Meaty Squash Pasta

Combining meats, vegetable, and starches makes a complete, well-balanced meal in one bowl—for baby and your entire family.

3 SERVINGS

¼ small unsalted butternut squash

½ cup cooked lean ground beef

¼ cup cooked pasta

1. Remove the seeds from the squash. Place facedown in a shallow pan of water. Bake for about 40 minutes at 400°F.

2. Allow to cool; then scoop out the squash flesh and place in food processor or blender.

3. Add beef and pasta.

4. Purée as needed to reach desired consistency. Thin with water if desired.

Blueberry Applesauce

FREEZER/SUPERFOOD

Add flavor to cooked apples by adding in other fruits. Serve this alone or add in oatmeal cereal for added fiber.

3 SERVINGS

1 medium apple, peeled and cored

½ cup fresh or frozen blueberries

⅛ teaspoon pure vanilla extract

¼ cup water

1. Cut apple into pieces and add to a medium saucepan.

2. Wash blueberries and place into the saucepan with the apple. Add vanilla and water.

3. Simmer over medium-low heat for about 25 minutes, or until the apple and berries are completely tender.

4. Transfer fruit to blender. Purée until mixture is semi-smooth, adding water if necessary.

The Best Superfood: Blueberries
According to research at Tufts University, blueberries are the stars of antioxidants. They contain the highest level of anti-oxidants in any food. Here's an interesting fact: As blueberries ripen, the amount of antioxidants in them may increase. Picking ripe blueberries to use in your dishes can boost the antioxidant capacity.

Raspberry-Pear Purée

FREEZER/SUPERFOOD/PARENTS

The hue of raspberries adds a splash of color to this dish, which your baby can enjoy any time of the year.

4 SERVINGS

1 medium apple

½ fresh pear

¼ cup raspberries

Water or breast milk for thinning as needed

1. Peel and core the apple, removing all seeds and skin. Cut into pieces and put into a saucepan.

2. Peel and core the pear. Cut into slices and add to the saucepan.

3. Wash raspberries and place into the saucepan along with the pear and apple. Cover with water and bring to a boil.

4. Simmer for about 25 minutes, or until the apple and pear are completely tender.

5. Put fruit into a food processor or blender. Purée until mixture is smooth, adding water or breast milk as necessary.

6. Pour the purée through a fine strainer to remove any seeds.

Don't Fall for Those Apples
Remember the old witch in the story of Snow White who tempted her to take a bite of a red, delicious, yet poisonous apple? Don't get tempted into purchasing conventionally grown apples because they rank high at number four on the Toxic Twenty list for pesticide load.

Garlic Mashed Potatoes

The fresh garlic adds a great flavor to potatoes. Make a big pot for all to enjoy. Top with Parmesan cheese if you dare! Yum.

8–12 SERVINGS

2 cups water

4 baking potatoes, peeled and chopped

1 garlic clove, pressed

Pat of unsalted butter

1. Add water and potatoes to a medium pot. Bring to a boil.

2. Add pressed garlic. Simmer over medium heat for about 10 minutes or until tender, stirring occasionally.

3. Remove potatoes with a slotted spoon and mash with a potato masher or fork. Add more water and mash until the potatoes are a smooth consistency, or purée in a blender.

4. Remove potatoes and add unsalted butter.

5. Serve warm. Freeze remaining portions.

Homemade Eco-Friendly Sanitizer

White distilled vinegar can wash away 99.99 percent of harmful bacteria, including E. coli, *Listeria monocytogenes*, and salmonella living on your kitchen counters and surfaces. Simply heat ½ cup vinegar in a pot until the temperature reaches 150°F. Pour the warm vinegar into a spray bottle and spray all kitchen surfaces and let stand for 1 minute. Wipe with a cloth. The vinegar must be heated for maximum effectiveness.

Twice-Baked Potatoes

Remember when your mother made twice-baked potatoes for dinner when you were younger? Here's a version that both you and baby can enjoy.

2 SERVINGS

1 baking potato

1 tablespoon mild Cheddar cheese

1 tablespoon shredded Parmesan cheese

Dab of unsalted butter

1. Bake potato in oven at 375°F for 30 minutes or until soft and tender.

2. Cut potato down the center, remove flesh, and mash up the inside with a fork. Top with cheese and a dab of unsalted butter.

3. Add mixture back into the potato. Bake an additional 5 minutes until cheese is melted.

4. Scoop out the potato and cheese from the skin. Mash with a fork and serve warm.

Cauliflower Casserole

This yummy dinner makes instant delicious baby food. The good part about it is that you are not purchasing anything extra, you're simply scooping out a little portion for your little one to enjoy. You'll probably still have leftovers! To make enough for your entire family double or triple this recipe.

4–6 SERVINGS

3 cups cauliflower, cut into florets

2 tablespoons unsalted butter

1⅓ cups tomatoes, skinned, deseeded, and roughly chopped

¼ cup Italian seasoned bread crumbs

¼ cup grated Parmesan cheese

¼ cup grated Cheddar cheese

1. Put the cauliflower florets in a steamer and cook until soft, about 12 minutes.

2. Meanwhile, warm unsalted butter in a pan, add tomatoes and bread crumbs, and sauté until mushy.

3. Remove from heat and add the cheeses, stirring until melted.

4. Mix the cauliflower with the mixture and blend to a semismooth consistency. Add water to thin if desired. Freeze remaining portions for up to eight weeks.

Pomegranate Glazed Carrots

This savory dish combines the sweetness from the carrots and agave nectar with the tartness of the pomegranate juice into a savory purée that the whole family can enjoy.

3 SERVINGS

1 cup fresh carrots, cut and peeled

½ cup 100 percent pomegranate juice

1 tablespoon agave nectar

1. Place carrots into a saucepan with enough water to cover them. Bring the water to a boil; then simmer until carrots are very tender, 15–20 minutes.

2. Drain the carrots and place into a blender or food processor. Purée for about 30 seconds.

3. Add water if necessary. Continue puréeing until smooth.

4. Pour juice in a small saucepan over medium-high heat. Cook for 15 minutes or until juice is reduced by half. Stir in agave nectar.

5. Combine agave glaze and carrot purée. Serve warm.

Blueberry Dream

Get two for one when you make this recipe and freeze in ice cube trays. Make an extra batch and freeze in festive ice cube tray molds, such as hearts or stars. Once the cubes are frozen, add them to sparkling lemonade or your favorite beverage for extra flavor and a powerful blend of antioxidants!

2 SERVINGS

1 cup blueberries

4 tablespoons water

¼ teaspoon pure vanilla extract

Rice cereal for thickening as needed

1. Combine all ingredients in a small saucepan.

2. Cook until blueberries start to burst open.

3. Purée until smooth. Use a sieve to remove any fibrous material if needed. Add rice cereal if desired to thicken. Serve.

Blueberry Cream Pie

FREEZER/SUPERFOOD/INSTANT/PARENTS

This delicious dessert purée introduces cream cheese, a soft white cheese that provides a great source of calcium, fat, and protein.

1 SERVING

4 tablespoons blueberries

1 tablespoon cream cheese

1 tablespoon crushed organic graham crackers, plain

1. Purée blueberries in a blender to a smooth consistency. Push through sieve to remove any fibrous material if necessary.

2. Combine blueberry purée and cream cheese. Fold in graham crackers. Serve immediately.

Simply Chicken Purée

BASIC/FREEZER

Using chicken or vegetable stock boosts the flavor of this purée. Use this purée in combination with other purées or serve alone.

4 SERVINGS

4 ounces boneless skinless chicken breast (about one small breast)

4 tablespoons homemade chicken or vegetable stock

1. Place chicken in a saucepan with a small amount of water, enough to almost cover the chicken. Cook over medium heat until completely cooked through, about 10 minutes.

2. Cut into small pieces and place in a blender.

3. Purée while gradually adding just enough broth or water to reach a smooth consistency.

Blueberry Pomegranate Parfait

When blueberries come into season, stock up on them and freeze them whole. Enjoy them all year round in smoothies, pies, and recipes like this one.

1 SERVING

4 tablespoons blueberries

1 tablespoon 100 percent pomegranate juice

2 tablespoons whole-fat plain or vanilla yogurt

1. Purée blueberries in a blender to a smooth consistency. Push through sieve to remove any fibrous material if necessary.

2. Combine blueberry purée and pomegranate juice. Fold in yogurt. Serve immediately.

Bananas Foster for Baby

A traditional bananas foster recipe includes caramel sauce, sugar, lemon juice, and brown sugar. Make this recipe for an organic remix suitable for baby.

1 SERVING

½ teaspoon unsalted butter

2 tablespoons crushed plain graham crackers

1 tablespoon agave nectar

½ small banana

⅛ teaspoon pure vanilla extract

1. Melt unsalted butter in a saucepan over medium heat. Add cracker crumbs and agave nectar. Stir and remove from heat.

2. Mash banana with fork. Combine all ingredients and serve.

Island Papaya Coconut

Nothing beats that warm island breeze except for the sweetness of this tropical purée. Leave out the rice cereal if you plan to freeze.

2 SERVINGS

4 tablespoons Hiya Papaya (Chapter 4)

2 tablespoons organic coconut milk or coconut water

2 tablespoons rice cereal

Combine all ingredients together. Thin with more coconut milk or water if desired. Serve immediately.

Cabbage Patch Purée

The cabbage in this recipe literally melts in your mouth it's so tender. For a meal the whole family can enjoy, double this recipe and serve with corned beef brisket!

10–12 SERVINGS

1 small head cabbage, washed and chopped

6 cups low-sodium chicken stock

2 tablespoons unsalted butter

½ cup chopped yellow onion

1. Add all ingredients to a large pot. Bring to a boil.

2. Simmer for 1 hour over medium-low heat, stirring occasionally.

3. Transfer cabbage to blender using a slotted spoon. Purée to a smooth consistency.

Apple and Plum Compote

Golden Delicious, Fuji, or Pink Lady apples make the best choices for this compote as they are sweeter than other varieties.

8 SERVINGS

1 sweet apple

2 small plums

⅛ teaspoon cinnamon

Enough water to cover fruit

1. Peel apple and plums and cut into chunks.

2. In a large saucepan, combine apple and plum chunks with cinnamon.

3. Cover fruit with water.

4. Cook until apples are very tender and start to break apart, approximately 10 minutes depending on the size of the chunks.

5. Mash with a potato masher or the back of a spoon. Transfer to blender or food processor if a finer consistency is needed.

Pumpkin Crème Pie

Pumpkin pie isn't just for big kids and older adults. Babies can have it, too! This recipe combines the autumn richness of pumpkins with a creamy yet crunchy bite.

2 SERVINGS

½ cup canned (nonsweetened) pumpkin or fresh pumpkin purée

2 tablespoons crushed graham crackers

1 tablespoon crème fraîche

Pinch of cinnamon

Combine all ingredients together and serve.

Gingered Pear Crisp

FREEZER

The ginger in this recipe adds a little kick to the pear. It's just enough to add flavor, but take care not to over-spice.

4 SERVINGS

⅛ teaspoon ground ginger

1 medium ripe pear, peeled, cored, and chopped

Crushed organic graham crackers, plain

1. Add ginger and chopped pears to a medium-sized saucepan.

2. Cover and cook on medium-low heat for about 7 minutes, until tender. Stir frequently.

3. Transfer the cooked pears to a blender.

4. Purée to a smooth consistency. Fold in graham crackers and serve immediately.

Chicken Parmesan

FREEZER/SUPERFOOD/PARENTS

Have Italian night at your home with Chicken Parmesan as the main course. All of the ingredients in this recipe can be set aside to make a version suitable for baby.

4 SERVINGS

¼ teaspoon Italian seasoning

½ cup tomato sauce, warmed through

½ cup cooked, unseasoned chicken, chopped

¼ cup linguine, broken into ½-inch pieces, cooked

2 tablespoons grated Parmesan cheese

1. Combine Italian seasoning and tomato sauce. Set aside.

2. Add chicken to blender. Purée until smooth, adding water when necessary.

3. Remove chicken. Combine with pasta and tomato sauce. Sprinkle with Parmesan cheese and serve.

Rosemary Cornish Hen Dinner

This is certainly a recipe that can be made for the entire family with portions taken out to purée for baby. Make sure to remove the skin on the Cornish hen before puréeing. However, season the hen with rosemary, garlic, salt, and pepper for the family!

3 SERVINGS

¼ cup broccoli florets

½ cup unseasoned Cornish hen, cooked and chopped

Pinch of dried rosemary

¼ cup mashed potatoes

1. Steam broccoli until tender, about 7–10 minutes.

2. Combine hen, rosemary, and broccoli together in a blender.

3. Purée to a semismooth consistency, adding water when necessary.

4. Fold in mashed potatoes. Serve. Refrigerate remaining portions for up to three days.

Rotisserie Chicken with Wild Rice

Save time on this recipe by purchasing a precooked organic rotisserie chicken from a grocery store that specializes in organic or whole foods. Purée baby's portion and have this dinner for the rest of the family.

4 SERVINGS

1 medium carrot

¼ cup cooked wild rice

½ cup cooked organic rotisserie chicken

1. Wash and peel the carrots. Cut into small pieces.

2. Place carrots in a saucepan with enough water to cover. Bring the water to a boil; then simmer until the carrots are very tender, about 15–20 minutes.

3. Place the carrots in a food processor or blender with the rice.

4. Dice chicken; add to the food processor.

5. Purée to a semismooth consistency, about 30 seconds, adding water when necessary.

Minted Peas

FREEZER/PARENTS

Don't know what to do with all the mint growing in your yard? Use some of it to make this minty recipe. Make and freeze big batches of this for later.

8 SERVINGS

2 cups frozen peas

½ teaspoon fresh or dried mint

Pat of unsalted butter

1. Steam peas until tender, about 10 minutes.
2. Transfer to blender. Add mint.
3. Purée while gradually adding water to reach a smooth consistency.
4. Top with unsalted butter and serve. Freeze remaining portions.

Cinnamon Peas Galore

FREEZER/PARENTS

Peas are a great first food that babies tend to enjoy. Give this recipe a try; even though it seems unusual, you'll be surprised! Serve this meal as a side dish to your family dinner. Instead of puréeing, serve the peas whole and top with unsalted butter and cinnamon.

8 SERVINGS

1 cup frozen peas

½ teaspoon cinnamon

Pat of unsalted butter

1. Steam peas over medium-high heat until tender, about 5–7 minutes.
2. Transfer to blender and add cinnamon.
3. Purée until smooth or mash with a fork. Add unsalted butter.
4. Serve warm. Freeze remaining portions.

Applesauce a la Raspberry

FREEZER/SUPERFOOD/PARENTS

Make flavored applesauce in bulk for the whole family to enjoy. Of course, baby will love it, but so will your pocketbook. Applesauce makes a great healthy snack and tastes great when combined with chicken.

4 SERVINGS

1 medium apple

½ cup raspberries

Water or breast milk for thinning as needed

1. Peel and core the apple, removing all seeds and skin. Cut into pieces and put into a saucepan.

2. Wash raspberries and place into the saucepan with the apple. Cover with water and bring to a boil.

3. Cover and simmer for about 30 minutes, or until the apples are completely cooked.

4. Put the fruit into a food processor or blender. Purée until smooth, adding water or breast milk as necessary.

5. Pour the purée through a fine strainer to remove any seeds from the raspberries.

Avocado and Kiwi Mash

SUPERFOOD/INSTANT

The kiwi in this recipe will add a boost of vitamins C and E to the avocado and an interesting taste. Pick a soft and plump kiwi to ensure it's ripe enough for baby. Cut a slice of avocado about 1-inch thick. Scoop fruit from skin.

3 SERVINGS

1 ripe avocado

1 ripe kiwi fruit

Breast milk as needed

1. Cut the kiwi in half and set aside half for a later meal. Using a spoon, scoop the fruit out of the shell. Cut off the central core and seeds. Put on a plate with the avocado.

2. Mash together with a fork until smooth. If needed, add a little breast milk for a creamier texture.

3. If the mixture is not smooth enough for your baby, purée in a food processor or blender until completely puréed.

Chicken and Apples

FREEZER

The apples dress up the chicken in this recipe and help create a delicious purée that can be enjoyed either hot or cold. Going on a family picnic? Pack up this dish in your cooler and pick a nice shady tree to sit under with your baby.

2 SERVINGS

1 small apple

½ cup cooked chicken

1. Wash and peel the apple; then cut into small pieces.

2. Place the apple in a saucepan and cover with water. Bring the water to a boil; then cook for about 20 minutes, or until the apple is very tender.

3. Combine the chicken and apple on a plate. Fork-mash until tender, or purée until semismooth.

4. If the mixture is too thick, add the leftover cooking water from the apple a little at a time until thinned.

Fruity Yogurt Parfait

SUPERFOOD/INSTANT

Instead of puréeing fruits, cut them into tiny pieces and add them to purées at this stage. At this point, your baby may want to experiment with chewing and self-feeding, so give her a spoon and let her have some fun!

2 SERVINGS

¼ cup ripe banana, **peach,** or **plum**

½ cup whole-fat vanilla yogurt

1. Remove the skin or peel from the fruit of your choice. Dice into small pieces, then fork-mash until smooth.

2. Layer yogurt, then fruit, then yogurt into a bowl for a baby parfait.

3. Serve immediately.

Melon Yogurt Chill-Out

Chill out by the pool and enjoy this refreshing treat with your baby. Feel the breeze as you mash up this purée on the spot for baby, without a blender! How cool. No equipment necessary. Make sure the melon is ripe enough for mashing.

1 SERVING

1 slice honeydew or cantaloupe

6 ounces whole-fat vanilla yogurt

1. Cut a thin slice of a ripe melon, removing any seeds. Slice the fruit off of the rind and fork-mash on a plate.

2. Blend in the yogurt with a spoon. Mix thoroughly.

Cinnamon Applesauce Yogurt

Save time purchasing plain organic applesauce from the store. Adding the cinnamon makes prepared applesauce taste more homemade.

2 SERVINGS

½ cup plain whole-fat yogurt

¼ cup prepared or homemade applesauce

Pinch of cinnamon

1. Stir the yogurt well to mix the creamy top layer with the rest of the yogurt.

2. Stir applesauce in with the yogurt.

3. Add a pinch of cinnamon and mix thoroughly.

4. Store leftovers in the refrigerator for up to two days.

Banana Apple Farina

Expand your baby's horizons by trying this recipe using farina, a creamy wheat cereal that's great for breakfast.

4 SERVINGS

1 cup water

3 tablespoons farina

½ very ripe banana

½ cup unsweetened applesauce

1. Bring the water to a boil. Add farina and stir well.

2. Reduce heat and cook until the farina thickens, about 1–3 minutes, stirring continuously. Remove from the heat and allow to cool for about 10 minutes.

3. Peel banana, removing any brown spots. Fork-mash until completely creamed.

4. Stir the applesauce and banana into the cooled cereal.

Banana Colada Ice

Pure coconut milk combined with organic bananas is a refreshing drink on a hot summer day. The coconut milk is lactose- and dairy-free and has more calcium than milk. So while you're out on the beach sipping on your colada, make sure your baby has hers too! Aaahhh! So healthy and refreshing.

1 CHILD AND 1 ADULT SERVING

1 cup unsweetened organic coconut milk

1 large banana

1 cup ice

1. Blend all ingredients together in a blender.

2. Serve in your baby's bottle or sippy cup.

Chicken Fontina with Blueberry Sauce

FREEZER/SUPERFOOD

This jewel-toned blueberry purée turns ordinary chicken into a delightful warm holiday meal for babies. This recipe can be made in advance and frozen. Or, you can easily blend this meal on the spot using unseasoned portions of the chicken or turkey you may already be having with blueberries.

2 SERVINGS

¼ cup frozen blueberries, thawed

½ cup cooked chicken, cubed

1 teaspoon fontina cheese (optional)

1. Add blueberries to blender and purée to a thin consistency.

2. Gradually add warm chicken, blending after each addition for a smooth consistency. For a chunkier purée, use the pulse function on your blender and pulse a couple of times. Sprinkle fontina cheese on top. Warm until melted. Stir and serve. Freeze remaining portions.

Sautéed Broccoli Purée with Parmesan Cheese

FREEZER/SUPERFOOD/PARENTS

Broccoli is high in fiber and vitamin C, so serve up this meal as a side dish to your baby's main course a few times per week. Double this recipe and combine all ingredients in a skillet and cook until broccoli is tender for the rest of the family.

4 SERVINGS

2 cups broccoli florets

1 tablespoon extra-virgin olive oil

½ tablespoon unsalted butter

2 tablespoons fresh grated Parmesan cheese

Water

1. Steam broccoli until tender in a double boiler.

2. Turn stovetop to medium-high heat. Coat the bottom of a sauté pan with extra-virgin olive oil. Add broccoli, unsalted butter, and Parmesan cheese and sauté for 5 minutes. Remove from heat.

3. Transfer sautéed broccoli and Parmesan cheese to blender. Purée. Gradually add water to reach a semi-smooth consistency.

Puréed Brown Rice

BASIC/FREEZER/SUPERFOOD

Hooray! After two months of simple rice cereal, do you think it's time for rice with more texture? Then make this recipe using brown rice. Your baby will get to enjoy mashing this with his gums. Feel free to serve this any time of day.

2 SERVINGS

¼ cup brown rice

½ cup water

Water or breast milk for thinning as needed

1. Combine the rice and water in a small saucepan. Bring to a rolling boil.

2. Cover the pot, turn down the heat to low, and simmer for 35 minutes, or until the water is completely absorbed.

3. Allow the rice to cool; then place into food processor or blender. Pulse for 30 seconds.

4. Add water or breast milk to thin if necessary.

Carrots and Brown Rice Medley

FREEZER/SUPERFOOD

Baby will love the tender-sweet taste of carrots in this healthy recipe.

3 SERVINGS

½ cup fresh carrots (1 medium-sized carrot)

2 tablespoons brown rice

¾ cup water

1. Wash and peel the carrot. Cut into 1-inch pieces.

2. Wash the rice to remove any dirt. Place into a medium saucepan, along with the carrots.

3. Add just enough water to cover the rice and carrots. Bring to a boil.

4. Reduce the heat to low. Cover the saucepan and simmer until most of the water is absorbed, about 20 minutes.

5. Place into a food processor or blender. Purée until smooth. Add more water if necessary.

Turnip and Sweet Potato Mash

FREEZER/SUPERFOOD/PARENTS

Turnips come in purple, white, and green. It doesn't matter which one you choose, they are all white on the inside!

1 SERVING

1 small turnip

⅛ cup water

4 tablespoons Simply Sweet Potato (Chapter 4)

1. Peel turnip and chop into small chunks.

2. In a small saucepan, combine turnip and water.

3. Bring to a boil and cook until the turnip is tender, approximately 10 minutes depending on the size of the chunks.

4. Transfer turnip to a blender. Purée until smooth.

5. Combine turnip purée with sweet potato purée.

Very Cherry-Chicken Rice Bowl

FREEZER/SUPERFOOD/PARENTS

This family-friendly dish makes an instant meal for your baby. If you plan on making chicken and rice for dinner, pan-fry a plain extra chicken breast to make a purée with a cherry on top for baby.

8 SERVINGS

2 tablespoons extra-virgin olive oil

1 boneless skinless chicken breast

½ cup pitted cherries

1 cup cooked brown rice

1. Add 2 tablespoons extra-virgin olive oil to a skillet.

2. Pan-fry chicken breast on both sides until insides are no longer pink, approximately 10 minutes.

3. Cut into small pieces and allow to cool.

4. Combine chicken, cherries, and brown rice.

5. Purée in a blender while gradually adding just enough water until desired consistency is reached. Freeze remaining portions.

Mango Chicken Feast

FREEZER

Save time by using frozen organic mangoes. They are equally nutritious as fresh.

8 SERVINGS

6 cups water

1 boneless skinless chicken breast

½ cup fresh mango, chopped

1. Bring 6 cups water to a boil in a large pot.

2. Place chicken breast in pot and boil until done, approximately 10 minutes.

3. Cut chicken breast into small pieces and allow to cool.

4. Purée in a blender with the mango; add just enough broth from cooking the chicken until desired consistency is reached. Freeze remaining portions.

Caribbean Chicken Dinner

SUPERFOOD

Bring on island flavor with this yummy delight. Make adult portions separately with Caribbean jerk seasoning, diced onions, curry powder, and fresh cilantro. Enjoy over brown rice and turn on some reggae music!

8 SERVINGS

6 cups water

1 boneless skinless chicken breast

1 small banana or ½ large banana

1 teaspoon organic coconut milk

1. Bring 6 cups water to a boil in a large pot.

2. Place chicken breast in pot and boil until done, approximately 10 minutes.

3. Cut chicken breast into small pieces and allow to cool.

4. Combine chicken, banana, and organic coconut milk.

5. Purée in a blender while gradually adding just enough broth from cooking the chicken until desired consistency is reached. Freeze remaining portions.

Papaya Chicken with Spice

FREEZER

Make sure the papaya you use is ripe enough. Otherwise, cut it into cubes and steam it until tender before puréeing.

8 SERVINGS

6 cups water
1 boneless skinless chicken breast
½ cup ripe papaya
Dash of nutmeg

1. Bring 6 cups water to a boil in a large pot.
2. Place chicken breast in pot and boil until done, approximately 10 minutes.
3. Cut chicken breast into small pieces and allow to cool.
4. Combine chicken, papaya, and nutmeg.
5. Purée in a blender while gradually adding just enough broth from cooking the chicken until desired consistency is reached. Freeze remaining portions.

Chicken-Parsnip Purée

FREEZER

The earthy flavor of parsnips pairs well with the chicken in this recipe. Add a little spice such as ginger or nutmeg for more flavor.

8 SERVINGS

1 medium-sized parsnip
1 cooked boneless skinless chicken breast
3 tablespoons water

1. Peel and dice parsnip.
2. Bring 1 cup water to a boil and cook parsnip until tender, about 15 minutes.
3. Cut cooked chicken into small pieces.
4. Combine chicken and parsnip.
5. Purée in a blender while gradually adding just enough water to achieve a semismooth consistency. Freeze remaining portions.

Chicken and Veggie Dinner

FREEZER/SUPERFOOD

The sweet onions introduce a savory flavor to this dish, making it a family favorite. This purée goes wonderfully with garlic mashed potatoes.

4 SERVINGS

1 boneless skinless chicken breast, chopped

1 small sweet onion, chopped

½ cup frozen peas

2 small carrots, chopped

2 teaspoons extra-virgin olive oil

1. Preheat oven to 350°F.

2. Add chicken, onion, peas, carrots, and olive oil to an 8" x 8" baking dish.

3. Bake for 15–20 minutes or until chicken is no longer pink and vegetables are tender.

4. Transfer baked ingredients, including broth to blender.

5. Purée until semismooth. Add water if necessary to thin.

Beef and Barley Blend

FREEZER/SUPERFOOD/PARENTS

While you're making beef and barley soup, take out these ingredients for baby.

2 SERVINGS

¼ cup ground beef, cooked

3 tablespoons cooked pearl barley

1 tablespoon yellow onion, chopped

⅛ teaspoon ground thyme

Organic vegetable broth

1. Combine cooked beef, barley, onion, and thyme together.

2. Purée in a blender while gradually adding just enough vegetable broth until desired consistency is reached. Serve warm.

Classic Pork Chop with Apples Purée

FREEZER/PARENTS

Apples and pork chop make an award-winning combination. If you don't have any frozen apple purée, use fresh cooked apples instead.

4 SERVINGS

1 boneless pork chop, cooked

1 cup Enchanting Apple
(Chapter 4)

1. Cut pork chop into small pieces.

2. Combine pork and apple purée together.

3. Purée in a blender. Gradually add water to thin if necessary to reach an age-appropriate consistency.

Poached Tilapia and Peaches

FREEZER/SUPERFOOD

Bake or sauté a cup of fresh peach slices if you don't have any frozen purée to use for this recipe.

4 SERVINGS

4 (7-ounce) tilapia fillets
(domestically farmed)

1 cup Just Peachy Purée
(Chapter 4)

1. Fill sauté pan with 1–2 inches water and bring to a boil.

2. Add fish fillets, cover, turn heat down to low, and allow to poach for 5–10 minutes.

3. Drain fish, saving small amount of liquid, and chop. Ensure no bones remain in fish.

4. Combine fish and peach purée.

5. Purée in a blender. Use broth from cooking the fish to reach an age-appropriate consistency.

Baby Gyro

Now your baby can have a taste of that wonderful Greek gyro dinner you love. Incorporate soft, little bites of pita bread into this purée for a full effect!

2 SERVINGS

2 ounces ground lamb

1 teaspoon extra-virgin olive oil

4 tablespoons cucumber, peeled, seeded, and chopped

2 tablespoons Greek yogurt, plain

1. Brown lamb in a medium saucepan with 1 teaspoon extra-virgin olive oil. Browning the lamb should take about 5 minutes for this small amount.

2. Remove lamb from pan and combine with the cucumber.

3. Purée in a blender to desired consistency. Add water to thin, if necessary.

4. Add mixture to a small dish and stir in yogurt. Add small pieces of soft pita bread if desired. Serve.

Heavenly Ham Purée

Use some of that heavenly ham from your holiday meal to make a purée. It's already cooked, so there's not much work involved! This purée goes great with mashed potatoes and even mashed corn muffins!

1 SERVING

½ cup cooked ham

3 tablespoons water

1. Chop precooked ham into small pieces.

2. Transfer to blender.

3. Purée while gradually adding just enough water to reach a smooth consistency.

"Where's the Beef?" Meal

BASIC/FREEZER/SUPERFOOD/PARENTS

You can tear off parts of the beef from the pot roast you already made instead of cooking the beef in this recipe. There's no need to buy extra beef for baby. It's more fun to share!

2 SERVINGS

4 ounces lean beef (rib roast or short loin)

3 tablespoons water or beef broth

1. Brown the beef in a pan until completely cooked through, typically 4–5 minutes per side for a thin steak. For a thicker piece, grill or roast until the interior temperature reaches 170°F.

2. Cut into small pieces and place in a blender.

3. Purée while gradually adding just enough broth or water to reach a smooth consistency.

Pilgrim's Feast Turkey Purée

BASIC/FREEZER/PARENTS

Use the leftover turkey from your holiday feast to whip up a nice turkey purée for baby. It's okay to purée even if the turkey is seasoned with mild spices or herbs. However, be careful of added salt.

1 SERVING

½ cup cooked, unseasoned skinless turkey meat

3 tablespoons water

1. Chop turkey into small pieces. Place in a blender.

2. Purée while gradually adding just enough water to reach a smooth consistency.

Special Veal

Veal tastes mild in flavor and comes from young cows. Add variety to this purée by adding soft pasta shapes or a few pinches of shredded cheese.

2 SERVINGS
• • • • • • • • • • •

1 tablespoon onion, minced

4 ounces lean veal

3 tablespoons water

1. Cook the onion over medium heat until translucent.

2. Add veal to the pan and fry until completely cooked, typically 4–5 minutes per side for a thin steak.

3. Cut into small pieces (less than 1-inch square) and place in a food processor or blender.

4. Purée while gradually adding just enough water to reach a smooth consistency.

Simply Lamb

A rare find in grocery aisles, this recipe expands your baby's palate with yet another flavorful meat. Babies can digest lamb easily and will benefit from all the iron it contains. Instead of using the oven, grilled lamb presents an even tastier treat.

2 SERVINGS
• • • • • • • • • • • •

4 ounces lean lamb

3 tablespoons water or broth

1. If using lamb chops, broil for 18–20 minutes, or until the meat reaches an internal temperature of 160°F. If using lamb shoulder or leg, roast at 325°F for 35–40 minutes.

2. Let the meat cool; then cut into small pieces and place in food processor or blender.

3. Purée while gradually adding just enough broth or water to reach a smooth consistency.

Basic Barley

This versatile, nutritious grain supports healthy brain development and offers baby a healthy dose of iron, vitamin C, phosphorous, magnesium, zinc, and potassium.

7–8 SERVINGS

1 cup pearled barley

3 cups water

1. Combine barley and water in a small saucepan and cover.
2. Simmer 45–55 minutes, or until barley is tender.

Quinoa

BASIC/SUPERFOOD/PARENTS

This healthy grain boasts fiber, essential amino acids, and protein. Before introducing quinoa, make sure your child can tolerate oatmeal, barley, and rice. Thoroughly rinse quinoa under running water.

8 SERVINGS

1 cup quinoa

2 cups water

1. Combine quinoa and the 2 cups water in a medium saucepan.
2. Bring to a boil.
3. Reduce heat, cover, and simmer for 15 minutes or until the outer ring of each grain separates.
4. Fluff before serving.

Squash and Corn Combo

FREEZER/SUPERFOOD

This recipe serves up the yellow color of the rainbow of foods. Make this purée smooth because of the corn. Check to make sure no indigestible fibers from the corn are present.

6 SERVINGS

½ cup peeled unsalted butternut squash chunks

½ cup water

¼ cup frozen sweet corn

1. Combine squash, water, and corn in a medium saucepan. Bring to a boil.

2. Stir frequently while cooking to ensure that squash cooks evenly.

3. Cook until tender, 8–10 minutes.

4. Transfer to a food processor or blender. Purée while gradually adding just enough water necessary to achieve a smooth consistency.

Autumn's Harvest Purée

SUPERFOOD

Take advantage of all the beta-carotene in this creamy and healthy dish. Use previously frozen purées to whip this up. Add spices like cinnamon and nutmeg for more robust flavor.

1 SERVING

2 tablespoons Enchanting Apple (Chapter 4)

2 tablespoons Pumpkin Patch Purée (Chapter 4)

2 tablespoons Simply Sweet Potato (Chapter 4)

Combine all ingredients in a bowl. Serve warm or cold.

Cinnamon–Apple–Sweet Potato Surprise

FREEZER/SUPERFOOD/PARENTS

The juices from baking the apple and sweet potato join together in this dish and are complemented by the wonderful taste and aroma of cinnamon.

1 SERVING

1 small apple, peeled, cored, and sliced

1 sweet potato, skinned and cubed

⅛ teaspoon cinnamon

1. Preheat oven to 350°F.

2. Combine apples, sweet potatoes, and cinnamon in an 8" x 8" square dish.

3. Bake for 40 minutes or until apple and sweet potato are nice and soft.

4. Purée in a blender with all the natural juices or fork-mash.

5. Serve warm.

Summertime Peach Raspberry Delight

FREEZER/SUPERFOOD/INSTANT/PARENTS

This charming dessert purée offers a dose of vitamin C and lycopene, which protects cells from damage.

6–8 SERVINGS

1 cup raspberries

5 small peaches, peeled, pitted, and chopped

1. Wash raspberries and drain, but do not dry.

2. Transfer moist raspberries and chopped peaches to a blender and purée until smooth

3. Pass purée through a fine-meshed sieve or strainer to remove raspberry seeds.

4. Freeze extra portions for up to eight weeks.

Peach Queen

SUPERFOOD/PARENTS

Quinoa, also known as the "Mother of All Grains," adds nice texture and a serving of whole grains to the smoothness of the peach purée. Quinoa offers iron, fiber, magnesium, and phosphorous, all essential for healthy development.

1 SERVING

4 tablespoons Just Peachy Purée (Chapter 4)

1 tablespoon cooked quinoa

Combine peach purée and cooked quinoa. Serve.

Secure the Feeding Bowl

Around ten months old, babies enjoy learning how to feed themselves. Sometimes this can become a messy feat, especially when her curiosity over the bowl peaks and she picks it up and tosses it across the room! Avoid this by purchasing feeding dishes that have suction cups at the bottom that can attach to highchair trays.

Sweet Peas with Orzo

FREEZER/PARENTS

The orzo pasta adds a good texture to this purée. Alternatively, you can substitute arborio rice for the orzo if you wish.

1 SERVING

2 tablespoons cooked orzo pasta

4 tablespoons Pretty Peas (Chapter 4)

1. Combine cooked orzo pasta and Pretty Peas purée.
2. If necessary, use a food processor or blender until desired consistency is reached.

Know Your Pasta

Although many mistake it for rice, orzo is actually pasta made from hard-wheat semolina. It makes a great substitute for arborio rice used in risotto and other recipes.

Baby Succotash

Corn offers a sweet flavor that appeals to many babies. This dish adds lots of texture because of the hulls of corn kernels. If the texture is too much, try offering this dish again in the third stage.

3 SERVINGS

½ cup lima beans (fresh or frozen)

½ cup fresh or frozen corn

2 cups water

1. Put the lima beans and corn into a saucepan. If using fresh corn, remove the husk and cut the kernels from the cob with a sharp knife.

2. Cover with the water; bring to a boil. Simmer until tender, about 15 minutes.

3. Put the beans and corn into a blender or food processor. Purée for 30 seconds.

4. Thin with the leftover cooking water and purée until semismooth.

5. For a creamier purée, thin with breast milk instead of water.

Pear-Apricot Mash

This purée is loaded with vitamin C, iron, potassium, and beta-carotene. Use dried apricots instead of fresh if you like.

3 SERVINGS

1 medium pear, peeled and cored

2 ripe apricots

2 cups water

1. Cut pear into chunks and place in a steamer basket.

2. Wash, halve, and remove the pit from the apricots. Place along with pear chunks in a steamer basket.

3. Add enough water so that it fills the pot under the steamer basket, about 2 cups. Bring to a boil and steam for 10 minutes, or until apricots are very soft.

4. Remove skins from apricots by scooping the fruit out with a spoon.

5. Place on a plate along with the pear and fork-mash fruit.

Sweet Potatoes and Peach Perfection

FREEZER/SUPERFOOD

The brilliant colors of orange in this recipe indicate an abundant presence of vitamin C and beta-carotene.

3 SERVINGS

½ small sweet potato
1 medium, ripe peach

1. Scrub the sweet potato and poke several holes in it. Bake at 400°F for 40 minutes.

2. Wash the peach and cut in half. Remove the pit and any of the harder inner fruit.

3. Scoop the peach out of the peel, or remove the peel with a paring knife. Place on a large plate.

4. When the sweet potato is cool, scoop the potato out of the peel and into a bowl. Combine with peach, and purée until semismooth.

Turkey and Cranberry Crush

FREEZER/SUPERFOOD

Because cranberries present a tart or sour flavor, adding the sugar or even agave nectar will help baby accept this purée. If you already have turkey and cranberries on the holiday table, grab a little and purée for baby.

4 SERVINGS

¼ cup water
½ tablespoon sugar
½ cup fresh or frozen cranberries
½ cup cooked turkey

1. Mix the water and sugar in a saucepan. Bring to a boil and cook at a high temperature for 2–3 minutes, stirring constantly.

2. Add cranberries. Reduce heat to a simmer; then cook for 15–20 minutes. Cranberries should burst, and the mixture will thicken.

3. Allow cranberries to cool completely. Meanwhile, dice turkey.

4. Purée all ingredients in a blender until semismooth. Add water if necessary.

Superstar Spinach Rotini

FREEZER/SUPERFOOD/PARENTS

If baby takes an interest in self-feeding, allow her to experiment with her hands. Make sure you cover the floor!

3 SERVINGS

¼ cup rotini pasta, chopped
1 cup fresh or frozen spinach

1. Place pasta in a pot and cover with water. Boil for 20–25 minutes, or until pasta is very tender.

2. If using fresh spinach, wash the leaves thoroughly, remove stems, and chop. Boil in a pan of shallow water for 10 minutes. If using frozen spinach, defrost and cook according to the package directions.

3. Transfer cooked spinach to a blender. Purée until smooth.

4. Stir in pasta. Serve warm.

Chicken and Broccoli Blend

FREEZER/SUPERFOOD/PARENTS

This easy recipe will make great use of a small portion of the chicken and broccoli you already plan on making! Top this off with a dab of unsalted butter for extra creaminess.

4 SERVINGS

1 cup broccoli florets, fresh or frozen
½ cup cooked chicken, diced

1. Add broccoli to steamer basket.

2. Add enough water to reach the bottom of the steamer basket. Bring to a boil; then cook for 15 minutes or until the broccoli is very tender.

3. Add chicken and broccoli to blender. Purée until semi-smooth. Add water if necessary. Serve warm.

Sweet Potato–Chicken Bake Purée

FREEZER/SUPERFOOD/PARENTS

If you already have previously frozen sweet potato or chicken purée, you'll save time by simply reheating and combining the two.

4 SERVINGS

1 small sweet potato, skinned and cubed

1 small boneless skinless chicken breast (about 6 ounces)

1. Preheat oven to 350°F.

2. Add sweet potato and chicken to a shallow dish. Bake for 20 minutes or until chicken is cooked thoroughly. It's okay if the sweet potato continues to bake.

3. After both chicken and potato have cooled, combine in a food processor or blender. Pulse until consistency is semismooth.

4. Serve warm.

Peachy Chicken Combo

FREEZER/PARENTS

Chicken tastes amazing when combined with flavorful fruits like apples and peaches. It also takes advantage of ingredients you have leftover from previous meals.

4 SERVINGS

½ cup cooked chicken, diced

½ very ripe peach, peeled and pitted

¼ cup white or brown rice, cooked

1. Combine chicken and peaches in blender. Purée until smooth. Remove.

2. Fold in rice. If mixture presents too much texture, fork-mash or purée to make it smoother.

3. Serve warm.

Beef and Carrot Mash

FREEZER/SUPERFOOD/PARENTS

Although babies' fat requirements are different than adults, look for at least 80 percent ground beef to accommodate the requirements of all family members. There's no need to purchase a separate package.

4 SERVINGS

½ small sweet onion, peeled and thinly sliced

½ cup lean ground beef

1 medium carrot, peeled and cut into ½-inch chunks

1 cup water

1. Sauté onion in a deep, nonstick pan until soft and translucent. Use extra-virgin olive oil to keep onions from sticking to the pan, if necessary.

2. Add the ground beef to the pan. Cook until browned.

3. Add carrots and water. Simmer on low heat for another 20 minutes, or until the carrots are tender.

4. Scoop mixture into a blender with a slotted spoon. Add a little cooking liquid. Pulse until semismooth. Serve warm.

Turkey–Sweet Potato Shepherd's Pie

FREEZER/SUPERFOOD/PARENTS

Consider using the dark pieces of turkey meat for puréeing in this recipe. Dark meat is juicer and more tender than white meat and makes a smooth purée. Alternatively, use leftovers to make this recipe.

4 SERVINGS

1 small sweet potato (or ½ large sweet potato), peeled and chopped

½ cup frozen corn

½ cup cooked turkey

1. Place sweet potatoes in a saucepan with the corn kernels.

2. Add enough water to cover. Bring the water to a boil; then simmer until the vegetables are very tender, about 15 minutes.

3. Place the corn, sweet potatoes, and turkey into a blender. Purée until semismooth.

4. Add cooking water, gradually, to make the mixture smoother, if necessary. This mixture will be somewhat thicker than other purées due to the corn kernels, so be sure that your baby is ready for the texture.

Veggie Pork Dinner

FREEZER/SUPERFOOD/PARENTS

As soon as the weather breaks, fire up the grill and invite your friends and their babies over for a grilled pork dinner—or purée!

4 SERVINGS

1 small baking potato (or ½ large potato)

½ cup green beans (fresh or frozen)

½ cup cooked pork, chopped

1. Wash and peel the potato. Cut into small pieces and place into a saucepan.

2. Break off the ends of the green beans (if fresh) and pull the strings off the sides. Cut into small pieces. Place in the saucepan with the potato pieces.

3. Add enough water to cover the potato and green bean pieces. Bring the water to a boil; then simmer until the potatoes and beans are very tender, about 15 minutes.

4. Place the beans, potatoes, and pork in a food processor or blender and purée for 30 seconds.

5. Add cooking water gradually to make the mixture smoother.

Beefy Peas and Potatoes

FREEZER/SUPERFOOD/PARENTS

Who said meat and potatoes had to be dull? Mix up the variety of potatoes in purées. Choose red skins or Yukon Gold to change things up!

3 SERVINGS

1 small baking potato (or ½ large potato)

½ cup peas (fresh or frozen)

½ cup cooked lean ground beef

1. Wash, peel, and dice potato. Place in a saucepan, cover with water, and boil for 10–15 minutes.

2. Add peas to saucepan. Boil for another 5–10 minutes until peas and potatoes are both very tender.

3. Let cool; then place in food processor with beef. Purée as needed to reach desired consistency, adding leftover cooking water to thin out the mixture.

"Real" Rice with Pear Purée

Celebrate baby's graduation from ground rice or boxed infant cereal with this heart-healthy purée.

3 SERVINGS
. . . .
½ **ripe pear**

½ cup water

¼ cup brown rice

1. Remove skin and core from pear, and chop into small pieces. Pour the water into a small saucepan. Bring to a rolling boil.

2. Add the rice and pears; then reduce to a simmer. Cook for 25–30 minutes or until all liquid is absorbed.

3. Purée to reach a semismooth consistency. Thin with water if desired.

Apricot Brown Rice

You can use previously frozen apricot purée in this recipe to make a quick meal for baby.

2 SERVINGS
. . . .
¼ cup brown rice

½ cup water

1 ripe apricot

1. Combine the rice with ½ cup water in a saucepan. Bring to a boil; then simmer for 20 minutes, or until all liquid has been absorbed.

2. Wash the apricot well. Peel it, remove the pit, and chop into small pieces.

3. Combine the rice and apricot in a food processor or blender. Purée until semismooth.

Lamb and Pumpkin Dinner

Sweet potatoes make a great substitute if you're all out of pumpkin—the sweetness and color are virtually the same.

4 SERVINGS
. . . .
1 teaspoon extra-virgin olive oil

2 ounces ground lamb

½ cup organic canned pumpkin

1. In a medium saucepan, add the teaspoon extra-virgin olive oil and lamb and brown lamb meat until done. Browning the lamb should take about 5 minutes for this small amount.

2. Remove lamb from pan and combine with the pumpkin.

3. Purée while gradually adding water to reach a smooth consistency.

Roasted Lamb and Tomato Compote

Use all of these ingredients to make a healthy meal filled with iron, lycopene, zinc, and beta-carotene for yourself.

2 SERVINGS
. . . .
2 ounces roasted lamb meat

¼ cup cooked brown rice

4 tablespoons Simply Sweet Potato (Chapter 4)

¼ cup diced tomatoes

Purée all ingredients in a blender or food processor.

Chickpea, Carrot, and Cauliflower Mash

FREEZER/SUPERFOOD/PARENTS

Reserve some of the chickpeas in this recipe to incorporate into a salad for yourself.

8 SERVINGS

2 carrots

1 cup cauliflower florets

2 cups cooked chickpeas (or 1 15-ounce can)

¼ cup vegetable broth or water

1. Peel and slice carrots.
2. Steam carrots and cauliflower until very tender.
3. Drain and rinse chickpeas.
4. Combine all ingredients and mash with a potato masher or fork.
5. Add broth or water as necessary to reach a semismooth consistency.

Rutabaga and Pear Medley

FREEZER

Rutabagas are beta carotene–rich root vegetables that grow best in cold climates, such as the northern United States and Canada.

4 SERVINGS

1 rutabaga

⅛ to ¼ cup water

1 small ripe pear, peeled, cored, and chopped

1. Peel rutabaga and cut off ends; cut into chunks.
2. Combine rutabaga and water in a small saucepan. Bring to a boil.
3. Boil until soft, approximately 10 minutes.
4. Transfer rutabaga, pear, and reserved cooking water to a blender. Purée until smooth. Add more water if necessary.

MENUS FOR EIGHT- TO NINE-MONTH-OLDS

Always introduce new foods separately to watch for signs of allergies. Once your baby has shown no reaction to the foods alone, you can introduce mixtures of foods. **EVERY DAY: Breast milk or formula:** 24–32 ounces per day

Iron-fortified infant cereal: ¼ cup per day

WEEK 1	MONDAY	TUESDAY	WEDNESDAY
	Pear Oatmeal	Fruity Yogurt Parfait	Mango Chicken Feast
	Rotisserie Chicken with Wild Rice	Garlic Mashed Potatoes	Cinnamon Peas Galore
	Pumpkin Crème Pie	Chicken and Apples	Baby-Style Beef Stew
THURSDAY	FRIDAY	SATURDAY	SUNDAY
Raspberry-Pear Purée with Basic Barley	Peach Queen	Avocado and Kiwi Mash	Banana Apple Farina
Pomegranate Glazed Carrots	Cauliflower Casserole	Very Cherry-Chicken Rice Bowl	Mango Chicken Feast
Blueberry Dream	Gingered Pear Crisp	Bananas Foster for Baby	Blueberry Cream Pie

WEEK 2	MONDAY	TUESDAY	WEDNESDAY
	Pear Oatmeal	Blueberry Pomegranate Parfait	Pear Oatmeal
	Broccoli and Cauliflower Bathed in Cheddar	Turnip and Sweet Potato Mash	Caribbean Chicken Dinner
	Applesauce a la Raspberry	Cinnamon Applesauce Yogurt	Puréed Collard Greens
THURSDAY	FRIDAY	SATURDAY	SUNDAY
Melon Yogurt Chill-Out with rice cereal	Banana Apple Farina	"Real" Rice with Pear Purée	Banana Apple Farina
Popeye's Spinach Meal	Baby Gyro	Turkey and Cranberry Crush	Cheesy Mashed Potatoes
Banana Colada Ice	Summertime Peach Raspberry Delight	Melon Yogurt Chill-Out	Blueberry Applesauce

WEEK 3	MONDAY	TUESDAY	WEDNESDAY
	Island Papaya Coconut	Melon Yogurt Chill-Out	Peach Queen
	Minted Peas	Papaya Chicken with Spice	Baby-Style Beef Stew
	Classic Pork Chop with Apples Purée	Apple Date Purée	Puréed Collard Greens

THURSDAY	FRIDAY	SATURDAY	SUNDAY
Pumpkin Patch Purée with Quinoa	Pear-Apricot Mash with rice cereal	"Real" Rice with Pear Purée	Banana Apple Farina
Avocado and Kiwi Mash	Classic Pork Chop with Apples Purée	Chicken and Broccoli Blend	Rutabaga and Pear Medley
Cinnamon–Apple–Sweet Potato Surprise	Cheesy Mashed Potatoes	Sweet Potatoes and Peach Perfection	Blueberry Pomegranate Parfait

WEEK 4	MONDAY	TUESDAY	WEDNESDAY
	Plum Delight with Quinoa	Melon Yogurt Chill-Out	Homemade Oatmeal Cereal with Blueberry Dream
	Special Veal; Minted Peas	Simply Lamb; Puréed Collard Greens	Simply Chicken Purée; Raspberry-Pear Purée
	Classic Pork Chop with Apples Purée	Island Papaya Coconut	Sweet Peas with Orzo

THURSDAY	FRIDAY	SATURDAY	SUNDAY
Pear Oatmeal	Blueberry Pomegranate Parfait	Fruity Yogurt Parfait	Banana Apple Farina
Pilgrim's Feast Turkey Purée; Cauliflower Casserole	Special Veal; Baby Succotash	Simply Chicken Purée; Sweet Peas with Orzo	Rutabaga and Pear Medley
"Where's the Beef?" Meal	Poached Tilapia and Peaches	Cinnamon Applesauce Yogurt	Blueberry Pomegranate Parfait

CHAPTER 6

PLEASING AN EXPANDED PALATE (TEN TO TWELVE MONTHS)
Chunky Purées for Little Ones

Your baby should be enjoying his journey in discovering new earthy tastes. By now, he's an experienced traveler, having discovered simple, smooth, sweet purées to thicker, seasoned meat purées. From ten months old, your baby can expand his palate to include more of nature's wonders, including strawberries, citrus, and teething biscuits (see Chapter 7). This chapter introduces fish, whole-wheat pasta, and pudding, foods that your baby is sure to enjoy and benefit from. The recipes in this chapter should be a chunky consistency, which can be achieved using the "pulse" action on a blender or by mashing the food with a fork. At this point, your baby can enjoy all of the purées in previous chapters and the transitional meals in Chapter 7 with the exception of cow's milk and honey if he's younger than twelve months. Therefore, encourage exploration and allow your baby to feed himself purées with his hands or with an infant fork or spoon. Keep plenty of bibs on hand!

It's been mentioned before, but it bears repeating: **Raw honey should not be given to a child under twelve months old.** It can cause a life-threatening illness called infant botulism. At this age, solid food should be offered three times per day with two snacks. Milk still plays an important part of your child's diet, and you should be giving your child 16–24 fluid ounces of breast milk or formula per day. Use previously frozen purées and combine them with pasta shapes, diced cooked vegetables, and yogurt, or use them as spreads for teething biscuits. Frozen purées can always be used, so don't let them go to waste!

THIRD-STAGE CUISINES: TEN TO TWELVE MONTHS

By now your baby should have a monster appetite, eating three meals and two snacks per day! Your baby has reached independence, an important step on the developmental ladder to feeding. Your baby should be able to tolerate a chunky texture and can begin to self-feed. Introduce the sippy cup, and allow him to drink more fluids. He should still continue to drink 16–24 ounces of breast milk or iron-fortified infant formula per day. Offer no more than 4 ounces of 100 percent no-sugar-added fruit juice per day. Expand the variety of cereals, fruits, vegetables, meats, soft breads, and finger foods. Babies will take about ¼–½-cup servings of each of these per day at this age.

The following list includes some new flavors and textures to add to your baby's diet:

- Black beans
- Breadsticks
- Couscous
- Citrus
- Diced vegetables (cooked)
- Dried fruit pieces
- Grits
- Pinto beans
- Plantains
- Rice cakes
- Strawberries

When introducing citrus and strawberries for the first time to your baby, watch out for stomach upset or other reactions. Most babies tolerate these foods well and can enjoy them at this age.

Atlantic Cod Dinner

FREEZER/SUPERFOOD/PARENTS

This oven-baked fish dinner provides super nutrition. Try it on a cool night while watching the sunset.

3 SERVINGS
. . . .

½ **medium carrot**

½ **small zucchini**

1 small Atlantic cod fillet

½ tablespoon unsalted garlic butter
(to make a batch, mix ½ cup softened,
unsalted butter with 1 tablespoon garlic
powder and 1 tablespoon dried parsley)

⅛ teaspoon lemon juice

1. Preheat the oven to 375°F. Wash and peel the carrot. Wash the zucchini; then cut both into thin slices.

2. Prepare a double layer of aluminum foil about 18" x 18", and lightly grease the inside of the foil.

3. Place the fish and vegetables in the foil, dot the top with unsalted butter and lemon juice, and then seal the packet and place in a baking dish. Bake for 45 minutes, or until the fish is opaque and flakes easily.

4. Allow to cool; then fork-mash before serving.

Baby Muesli

SUPERFOOD/PARENTS

The breakfast cereal muesli, which means "mixture" in German, was first created by a Swiss nutritionist as a health food. Feel free to substitute different fruits and grains.

2 SERVINGS
. . . .

½ ripe banana

1 ripe pear

2 ripe apricots

¼ cup regular oats (not quick-cooking)

1 cup milk (or soy milk)

1. Peel the banana, pear, and apricots. Remove all stems, seeds, and pits.

2. Chop into small pieces.

3. Pour the oats and milk into a saucepan. Bring to a boil; then cook at a boil for about 30 seconds.

4. Add in the fruit pieces and stir thoroughly.

5. Cover the pot, turn down the heat to low, and simmer for 8–10 minutes, or until the oats are smooth and thick. Stir occasionally to prevent sticking and burning.

6. Serve as is or purée for a creamier texture.

Tofu Veg Stir-Fry

Because soy sauce is high in sodium, choose a light or low-sodium variety and stay away from the bouillon cubes. Use fresh or prepared chicken stock instead.

2 SERVINGS

1 small carrot

2 large broccoli florets

½ small zucchini

2 ounces firm tofu

2 tablespoons extra-virgin olive oil

1 teaspoon light soy sauce

¼ teaspoon garlic powder

⅛ teaspoon ginger, ground

1 cup chicken stock or water

1. Wash the vegetables well. Peel the carrot; then dice all vegetables into small pieces.

2. Cut the tofu into small strips.

3. Heat the oil in a large frying pan. Add the tofu and stir-fry until brown, about 5 minutes.

4. Add vegetables, soy sauce, garlic powder, ginger, and stock. Bring the stock to a boil; then stir-fry until all vegetables are cooked and tender, about 12–15 minutes.

5. Allow to cool; then fork-mash before serving if desired.

Types of Tofu

Tofu comes in many varieties: silken or soft, firm, and extra-firm. When following a tofu recipe, pay attention to the type of tofu it calls for. Silken tofu is best for puddings and dips, while stir-fries mostly use firm tofu.

Captain's Fish Chowder

All aboard! This thick and creamy soup offers a serving of vegetables and the catch of the day, tilapia.

2 SERVINGS

½ medium white potato, diced

⅛ cup corn

⅛ cup peas

2 cups water

1 small tilapia fillet

1 tablespoon unsalted butter

¼ cup milk (regular or soy)

1. Combine potato, corn, and peas in a saucepan with 2 cups water.

2. Bring to a boil; then cook for 25 minutes, or until the potatoes are soft.

3. Wash the fish fillet, removing any bones. Place fish into the bottom of a microwave-safe dish and add enough water to cover the bottom of the dish. Cover with either a lid or microwave-safe plastic wrap.

4. Cook fish in the microwave on high for 3 minutes. Let rest; then cook for another 3–4 minutes. Fish is done when it flakes easily with a fork and is an opaque color.

5. Drain the vegetables. Add the fish, unsalted butter, and milk, stirring over low heat until the chowder thickens. Allow to cool; then fork-mash or purée before serving.

Which Fish Are Safe?

The Shedd Aquarium in Chicago produces a "Right Bite" guide to fish consumption. This guide shows you which fish are abundant, well cared for, and caught or farmed in environmentally friendly ways. Tilapia farmed in the United States is a best choice on this list and is not at risk for high mercury content.

Parmesan-Crusted Chicken

FREEZER/SUPERFOOD/PARENTS

This is one of those meals that can be prepared for the whole family. This recipe makes enough for three adults in addition to three servings for your baby. Make a side of fresh or frozen broccoli to enjoy with your meal.

3 ADULT SERVINGS;
3 BABY SERVINGS

Nonstick cooking spray

1 cup Italian bread crumbs

1 cup freshly grated Parmesan cheese

½ cup diced scallions

4 boneless skinless chicken breasts (uncooked)

1 cup milk

8 tablespoons Sautéed Broccoli Purée with Parmesan Cheese (Chapter 5)

1. Generously spray baking dish with nonstick cooking spray.

2. Combine bread crumbs, cheese, and scallions in shallow dish.

3. Dip each chicken breast in milk and then coat both sides with cheese mixture.

4. Place each breast in baking dish and spray the top with cooking spray.

5. Bake for 20–25 minutes at 375°F.

6. Cut chicken into cubes and add to food processor or blender and purée to a chunky consistency. Remove chicken from blender and add the Sautéed Broccoli Purée with Parmesan Cheese. Freeze remaining portions.

Baby's Cordon Bleu

FREEZER/PARENTS

Use a meat pounder or mallet for tenderizing the meat when stuffing chicken or beef. Meat mallets come in both wood or metal. Simply wrap the meat in plastic wrap on an appropriate work surface, and pound it with the mallet. Using the plastic wrap helps reduce contamination on surfaces.

2 SERVINGS

1 small boneless skinless chicken breast (about 6 ounces)

2 thin slices of ham

2 ounces Swiss cheese, shredded

1 tablespoon unsalted butter, melted

2 tablespoons bread crumbs

1. Preheat the oven to 350°F. Wash the chicken breast and remove any skin or fat.

2. Slice the chicken breast in half horizontally. Pound with a meat mallet to make the chicken as thin as possible.

3. Place the ham slices over one piece of chicken. Sprinkle the cheese on top; then place the other piece of chicken on top.

4. Place the assembly in a greased baking dish. Brush with melted unsalted butter and sprinkle the top with bread crumbs. Bake for 40 minutes, or until the chicken's internal temperature reaches 170°F. The juice from the chicken should run clear when pricked with a fork.

5. Allow to cool. Fork-mash or use a blender to pulse for a chunky consistency.

Black Beans

BASIC/SUPERFOOD/PARENTS

Black beans provide fiber, protein, and powerful antioxidants. Give your baby a dose of this chunky purée a few times per week. Mix it with other frozen purées in your freezer stash for a fresh take on a classic.

8 SERVINGS
....

1 cup dried black beans (or 1 15-ounce can of black beans)

3–4 cups water (or enough to cover beans)

1 tablespoon extra-virgin olive oil

1. Soak dried beans in enough water to cover, according to package directions, for 6–8 hours or overnight before cooking.

2. Drain soaking water from beans and rinse.

3. In a medium saucepan combine beans with enough water to cover and bring to a simmer with the lid tilted.

4. Cook 1–1½ hours or until tender.

5. Drain and rinse cooked beans (or drain and rinse canned beans, if using).

6. In a medium saucepan or sauté pan, heat extra-virgin olive oil over medium heat.

7. Add beans and heat through for 1–2 minutes, or until desired temperature is reached.

8. Remove from heat and mash beans with a potato masher or fork.

Super Duper Black Beans

Black beans contain the same amount of antioxidants as grapes and cranberries. The darker the beans, the more antioxidants they contain. Looking for an iron-rich food for your baby? Look no further than black beans. They contain almost 4 grams of iron per cup of black beans.

Oatmeal with Sautéed Plantains

SUPERFOOD/PARENTS

This hearty recipe makes great use of plantains and can be made for breakfast any day of the week for everyone in the family.

4 SERVINGS

1 yellow plantain (very ripe)

1 tablespoon brown sugar

1 teaspoon unsalted butter

½ cup water

½ cup 100 percent apple juice

⅔ cup rolled oats

1 teaspoon ground cinnamon

1. Peel and cut plantain into ½-inch pieces.

2. Put brown sugar in plastic bag and place plantain pieces in bag, shaking the bag to coat them.

3. Heat unsalted butter in small pan over medium heat, place plantains in pan, and cook until the sugar begins to caramelize, about 2 minutes each side; remove from heat.

4. In a small saucepan, combine water and apple juice. Bring to a boil.

5. Once boiling, stir in rolled oats and cinnamon. Return to a boil.

6. Reduce heat to low and simmer to desired thickness, 3–5 minutes.

7. Top oat mixture with mashed plantains and serve.

Plantains Versus Bananas

Plantains are firmer and have a lower sugar content than bananas. Plantains need to be cooked, but bananas are mostly eaten raw. In tropical areas of the world, plantains are often a first food for babies. Plantains are a staple item in these areas and are consumed on a daily basis.

Refried Pinto Beans

Make this classic recipe as a side dish—it goes well with rice (see Pinto Beans and Brown Rice recipe later in this chapter).

8 SERVINGS

1 cup dried pinto beans (or 1 15-ounce can)

3–4 cups water (or enough to cover beans)

1 tablespoon extra-virgin olive oil

½ onion, finely chopped

1 clove garlic, minced

1 teaspoon cumin

1. Soak dried beans in enough water to cover, according to package directions, for 6–8 hours or overnight before cooking.

2. Drain soaking water from beans and rinse.

3. In a medium saucepan, combine beans with enough water to cover, and bring to a simmer with lid tilted.

4. Cook 1–1½ hours or until tender.

5. Drain and rinse either cooked beans or canned beans, if using.

6. In a medium saucepan or sauté pan, heat extra-virgin olive oil over medium heat.

7. Add onion and garlic.

8. Cook until onion is tender, 3–5 minutes.

9. Add beans and cumin, and heat through for 1–2 minutes, or until desired temperature is reached.

10. Remove from heat, and mash with a potato masher or fork.

Fresh Strawberry Yogurt

SUPERFOOD/INSTANT/PARENTS

There's no need to purchase strawberry yogurt when your baby can have yogurt with freshly puréed straw-berries. Purchasing vanilla yogurt gives you more flexibility to add any kind of puréed fruit your baby enjoys.

1 SERVING

6 ounces whole-milk yogurt, plain or vanilla

1 strawberry, hulled and puréed

Combine all ingredients and serve immediately.

Strawberry and Cantaloupe Joy

FREEZER/INSTANT/PARENTS

Cantaloupe and strawberries make a joyful combination for teething babies. The soft texture of cantaloupe is soothing on a baby's gums. You can also soothe baby's gums by freezing this purée and making a sorbet. Make sure the cantaloupe is fully ripe for best results.

2 SERVINGS

2 strawberries, hulled and cut in quarters

1 cup chopped ripe cantaloupe

Combine all ingredients in a blender. Pulse blender a few times for a chunky purée.

Minted Bananas and Strawberries

You can't go wrong with bananas and strawberries. Liven up the combination with a touch of fresh mint. Look for mint in the produce aisle at the grocery store.

4 SERVINGS

1 pint fresh strawberries

1 large banana

10 large fresh mint leaves

1. Rinse strawberries and remove hulls (leaves and central core) with a sharp knife. Cut into pieces.

2. Peel banana, removing any brown spots. Cut into pieces.

3. With a sharp knife, cut the mint leaves into thin strips.

4. Place all ingredients in a steamer basket. Place in a pot over about 2 inches of water. Bring to a boil, and steam for about 5 minutes. Remove fresh mint leaves.

5. Serve in pieces, or mash to desired consistency.

Frutti-Tutti Tofu

Silken tofu makes puréeing easy. Firmer bean curds may need additional liquid and may not be as smooth. Remember to look for tofu made with non-GM soybeans.

1 SERVING

1 large strawberry

1 ounce silken tofu

1. Wash the strawberry and remove the stem.

2. Combine the tofu and the strawberry in a food processor or blender. Purée until smooth.

Freezing Tofu
Freeze leftover tofu in small containers or ice cube trays. Freezing and thawing it tends to cause better absorbency, although adults may frown at the soggier texture. However, baby will love it!

Wild Bananas 'n' Cream

SUPERFOOD/INSTANT/PARENTS

Baby will go wild for this delicious dessert! Try adding cinnamon and a pinch of sugar for the rest of your crew. The light cream makes it healthier for everyone to enjoy without worrying about packing on pounds. However, just like with most things, allow your baby to enjoy this in moderation and not more than twice per week.

2 SERVINGS
....

1 ripe banana

¼ cup light cream

1. Peel the banana, removing any brown spots. Cut into slices and place in food processor or blender.

2. Add cream.

3. Purée to desired consistency. If desired, add more cream to make a smoother purée.

4. If your baby likes his food with more texture, fork-mash instead of using the food processor.

Bananas and OJ

SUPERFOOD/INSTANT/PARENTS

This recipe, rich in potassium and vitamin C, also tastes great as a smoothie. Look for signs of citrus allergies as you introduce your child to oranges for the first time.

1 SERVING
....

Juice of 1 medium orange

1 ripe banana

1. Slice the orange in half. Juice it using either a juicing machine or a manual juicer. You can also simply squeeze firmly over a bowl. Strain out any pulp or seeds.

2. Peel the banana, removing any brown spots. Cut into slices and place on a plate.

3. Fork-mash the banana, slowly adding in the orange juice. Continue mashing until the texture is such that your baby can eat it with a spoon.

Potato Parsnippets

FREEZER

Yukon Gold potatoes offer an unsalted buttery-rich flavor and creamy texture. Remember to get medium-sized parsnips for better flavor.

6 SERVINGS
. . . .
4 Yukon Gold potatoes
2 medium-sized parsnips
Water to cover
1 tablespoon extra-virgin olive oil
¼ teaspoon salt (optional)

1. Peel potatoes and parsnips.
2. Roughly chop vegetables and place in a medium saucepan.
3. Cover with water.
4. Bring mixture to a boil; then reduce heat to a simmer.
5. Cook until vegetables are tender, approximately 10–15 minutes depending on size of chopped pieces.
6. Drain, reserving cooking liquid.
7. Return vegetables to pot, mash with a potato masher or fork, stir in extra-virgin olive oil and salt (if using).
8. Add reserved cooking water, 1 tablespoon at a time, until mash is the desired consistency.

Pineapple Cabbage

If your baby isn't sure about this dish, try offering it at another time. It may take awhile before a child accepts new tastes and textures, but it's certainly worth the effort!

5–8 SERVINGS
. . . .
½ head green cabbage
½ cup 100 percent pineapple juice
½ tablespoon unsalted butter

1. Slice cabbage and cook in a large saucepan over medium heat with pineapple juice. Cover. Cook for 20 minutes or until tender.
2. Remove cabbage with a slotted spoon. Purée in blender with butter until you reach a smooth consistency.

Indian Rice Pudding

FREEZER

This popular Indian dish ensures that your baby gets both the carbohydrates and calcium he needs for energy and strong bones. Ideally, use white rice because brown rice takes longer to cook and may come out too thick.

2 SERVINGS

½ cup white rice

1 cup water

1 cup milk (or soy milk)

1. Put rice and water in pan. Heat to boil; then reduce heat and simmer until water is absorbed, about 20 minutes for white rice.

2. Once rice is cooked, add milk to the pan and mix well.

3. Cook at medium heat for 10 minutes, stirring often. Mixture will thicken.

4. Allow mixture to cool and mash with fork to desired consistency. Serve lukewarm.

Apples 'n' Cream

FREEZER/PARENTS

After going apple picking, make this dessert for baby. Choose Fuji, Pink Lady, or Gala apples for a sweet dessert. Top this off with cinnamon or nutmeg if you like.

2 SERVINGS

1 apple, peeled, cored, and cut into 1" pieces

½ cup water plus more as needed

¼ cup milk (or soy milk)

1. Place apple pieces in small pan with water—water should almost cover apple pieces.

2. Bring to a boil; then simmer over low heat until apple pieces are tender, about 10 minutes. Check while cooking to make sure that there is still water left, and add more water while cooking if necessary.

3. When cooked, remove apples from heat. If there is a lot of excess water, drain off.

4. Add milk to pot and mash with a fork or potato masher until desired consistency, mixing well.

Baby Ratatouille

Ever see the animated movie Ratatouille, where this brilliant rat becomes a famous chef? You'll become famous after making this French vegetable stew for your family!

4 SERVINGS

1 tablespoon extra-virgin olive oil

½ small onion, diced

½ small eggplant, diced

1 small zucchini, diced

16-ounce can stewed tomatoes

½ teaspoon oregano

½ teaspoon parsley

½ teaspoon basil

1. Heat the oil in a medium saucepan. Sauté onion until it begins to brown and turns translucent.

2. Add the eggplant, zucchini, and tomatoes into the saucepan. Bring to a boil; then reduce to a simmer.

3. Cook for 20 minutes. Stir in the herbs; then cook for another 20 minutes. Allow to cool; then fork-mash before serving.

Tomato and Mushroom Pasta

Tomatoes grow effortlessly in a pot or backyard with hundreds of varieties to choose from. If you have a few vines growing, pick a ripe tomato off for this recipe.

2 SERVINGS

2 cups water

½ cup pasta

1 teaspoon extra-virgin olive oil

¼ cup white button mushrooms

1 medium, fresh tomato

⅛ teaspoon basil

1. Bring the water to a boil in a medium saucepan. Add the pasta, then cook for 10–15 minutes, or until pasta is very tender.

2. Heat the oil in a small frying pan. Sauté the mushrooms for 6–7 minutes, or until tender.

3. Wash and dice the tomato, removing the stem and any tough white parts. Add to the frying pan with basil and sauté for 15–18 minutes, or until very tender.

4. Drain pasta and toss with the mushroom-tomato mix.

5. Allow to cool; then fork-mash before serving.

Asian Chicken Fried Rice

Give your baby a taste of Asian fare with this quick and easy fried rice recipe. This recipe also works well with beef.

2 SERVINGS
. . . .

½ tablespoon sesame oil

½ boneless skinless chicken breast (about 4 ounces), cooked and diced

¼ cup cold brown rice, cooked

2 tablespoons fresh sweet peas (or frozen, thawed peas)

1. Over medium heat, add oil to skillet.

2. Add chicken, rice, and peas. Sauté for about 5 minutes. Remove from heat.

3. Fork-mash or add to blender and pulse for a chunky purée. Add water to thin.

Mild Chicken and Coconut Curry Purée

Add a little color of green to this recipe with a sprig of parsley or broccoli florets for a beautiful presentation.

3 SERVINGS
. . . .

1 tablespoon mild red curry paste

1 teaspoon extra-virgin olive oil

½ boneless skinless chicken breast (about 4 ounces), diced

1 small white potato, diced

½ cup coconut milk

1 cup chicken stock or water

1. Cook the curry paste and oil in a medium saucepan for 2–3 minutes, watching carefully to make sure it doesn't burn.

2. Add chicken to curry and brown the chicken for 3–4 minutes.

3. Add potato, coconut milk, and chicken stock to the saucepan.

4. Simmer for 25–30 minutes, or until the potato and chicken are cooked through. Stir occasionally to prevent sticking.

5. Allow to cool; then fork-mash before serving.

Garlic Asparagus with Parmesan

Here is a tasty asparagus recipe for your baby. The extra-virgin olive oil and garlic really boost the nutritional value of this vegetable and provide the fatty acids needed to promote healthy brain development. Skip the purée step when serving for the family.

2 SERVINGS

6 fresh asparagus spears, trimmed
½ tablespoon extra-virgin olive oil
¼ cup grated fresh Parmesan cheese
1 garlic clove, pressed
Water

1. Place asparagus in a baking dish and drizzle with extra-virgin olive oil. Add Parmesan cheese and garlic.

2. Bake asparagus at 400°F for 20 minutes or until tender.

3. Remove from oven and cut spears into thirds. Purée while adding water to achieve a chunky consistency.

First Rice Pudding

You can use leftover rice in this recipe instead of preparing it from scratch. Simply combine the leftover rice with the other ingredients and bake at 350°F for 45 minutes.

3 SERVINGS

1¼ cups milk (regular or soy)
½ cup white rice
2 teaspoons white or brown sugar
¼ teaspoon vanilla extract

1. Bring 1 cup milk and rice to a scalding point (watch carefully so the milk doesn't boil).

2. Reduce to a simmer; then cook for 30 minutes, or according to package directions. Rice is done when the liquid is absorbed and rice is fluffy.

3. Give the rice a good stir. Add sugar, vanilla, and ¼ cup milk.

4. Simmer over low heat for about 10 minutes, or until the liquid is mostly absorbed.

5. Allow to cool; then fork-mash or purée before serving.

Bread Pudding Bonanza

SUPERFOOD/PARENTS

Use leftover bread for this recipe, even if it's gone stale. The baking process softens it up and offers a nice texture that's easy for baby to eat. Serve your portion with caramel or chocolate sauce on top!

2 SERVINGS

4 slices bread

1 egg

½ cup evaporated milk

1 tablespoon melted unsalted butter

3 tablespoons brown sugar

½ teaspoon vanilla extract

¼ teaspoon cinnamon

1. Preheat the oven to 350°F.

2. Cut the bread into cubes and place in the bottom of a greased ovenproof baking dish.

3. Mix the egg, evaporated milk, unsalted butter, sugar, vanilla, and cinnamon into a bowl. Pour over the bread cubes and let it soak for 10–15 minutes.

4. Bake for 45 minutes, or until a toothpick inserted into the center comes out clean.

Baby's Homemade Apple Pie

FREEZER

This recipe offers all the flavors of a traditional apple pie, except it's just for baby. Use any sweet variety of apples for this recipe.

2 SERVINGS

1 red Gala or Fuji apple

1½ cups water

⅛ teaspoon fresh lemon juice

1 teaspoon brown sugar

⅛ teaspoon cinnamon

Organic graham crackers, crushed

1. Wash, peel, and core the apple. Chop into small chunks.

2. Put apple pieces in a small saucepan with 1½ cups water, lemon juice, brown sugar, and cinnamon. Bring to a boil; then simmer for 25 minutes, or until apple is very soft. Stir occasionally.

3. Fork-mash. Top with a heap of crushed graham crackers and serve.

Baby's Peachy Cobbler

The shortbread cookies replace the traditional sweet biscuit or pie crust topping found in peach cobbler.

2 SERVINGS

1 fresh peach

1 teaspoon brown sugar

⅛ teaspoon cinnamon

Organic shortbread cookies, crushed

1. Preheat oven to 350°F.

2. Wash the peach and cut into thin slices. Remove the skin.

3. Place peach into a small greased baking dish with brown sugar and cinnamon. Give it a quick stir; then bake for 30 minutes, or until peaches are completely soft.

4. Remove from oven. Fork-mash. Top with a heap of shortbread cookies.

Easy-Peasy Pear Dessert

For a grown-up variation, serve this on top of vanilla ice cream or pound cake.

1 SERVING

1 pear

2 teaspoons melted unsalted butter

⅛ teaspoon cinnamon

2 teaspoons brown sugar

1. Peel and core the pear. Dice into small pieces and mix with unsalted butter, cinnamon, and sugar.

2. Bake in a baking dish at 350°F for 30 minutes, or until pear is soft to touch.

3. Fork-mash and serve.

Baked Apples

This classic dessert will appeal to everyone, especially baby. The cinnamon and sugar bake right inside of the apple, a nice change from slicing the fruit and mixing it with sugar and spice.

1 SERVING

1 apple

1 teaspoon white sugar

⅛ teaspoon cinnamon

¼ cup water

1. Preheat the oven to 350°F. Wash the apple. Remove the top core, leaving the apple intact.

2. Sprinkle sugar and cinnamon on the inside of the apple. Pour the water into a small baking dish; then place the apple in the center. Bake for about 45 minutes, or until the apple is completely cooked.

3. When cooled, fork-mash to a suitable consistency. If desired, the entire skin can be removed once the apple is cooked.

Baked Zucchini

Pizza, pizza! Not quite! This recipe resembles pizza, but it's a healthier alternative in disguise. Season with salt and pepper for older members of the household.

2 SERVINGS

1 medium zucchini

½ cup tomato sauce

½ cup shredded mozzarella

1 tablespoon oil

1. Preheat the oven to 350°F. Scrub the zucchini and trim both ends. Slice into rings.

2. Place zucchini into a baking dish. Smother with tomato sauce and mozzarella and oil; then cover the dish.

3. Bake for 45 minutes, or until zucchini is very soft and cheese is melted. Serve as is or fork-mash if desired.

Chicken and Spinach Stir-Fry

Stir-frying is a quick, easy, and healthy way to cook for children. Use a nonstick skillet for stir-fries, or if you have a wok, give it a try! If the vegetables seem too crisp, try adding more liquid to soften things up a bit.

2 SERVINGS

1 small boneless skinless chicken breast (about 6 ounces)

1 tablespoon extra-virgin olive oil

1 cup fresh spinach (or ¼ cup precooked)

½ cup chicken stock or water

¼ teaspoon parsley

1. Wash the chicken breast and remove any fat. Dice into small pieces.

2. Heat the oil in a nonstick skillet or wok. Add the chicken and stir-fry for 8–10 minutes or until chicken is no longer pink in the middle.

3. Add the spinach, chicken stock, and parsley. Continue to stir-fry an additional 4–5 minutes.

4. Allow to cool; fork-mash and serve.

Ham and Peaches

Because honey can only be served to children who are twelve months and older, agave nectar offers a sweet substitute for those younger than twelve months.

1 SERVING

½ ripe peach

3 ounces ham, cooked

1 tablespoon unsalted butter

1 teaspoon agave nectar

1. Wash the peach and cut in half. Peel the half you're using for this recipe, remove the pit, and dice into small pieces. Either cut a wedge out of a ham steak or use 2 thin slices of cooked nitrate-free deli-style ham.

2. Melt the butter in a skillet. Add the ham and sauté for several minutes, or until both sides are lightly browned. Add the agave nectar and cook another 1–2 minutes.

3. Add the diced peach to the skillet. Cook for 4–5 minutes, stirring constantly to prevent sticking or burning.

4. Allow to cool; fork-mash and serve.

Silly Dilly Poached Salmon

FREEZER/SUPERFOOD/PARENTS

Poaching, a healthy and easy way of cooking, locks in flavor and will keep the fishy smell out of your kitchen. Try infusing flavor into the water by adding spices like salt and pepper, parsley, or even lemon juice. However, remove those ingredients before serving.

2 SERVINGS

1 thin salmon fillet

2 tablespoons water

Dash of dried dill

1. Wash the salmon well, removing all bones.

2. Pour the water and dill into a sauté pan. Place the fish into the pan, putting the skin side facing down.

3. Bring the water to a boil. Reduce to a simmer, cover the pan, and cook for 10–12 minutes or until the fish flakes easily with a fork.

4. Allow to cool; then do one more check for bones. Either serve as is or fork-mash if desired.

Good Old-Fashioned Oatmeal

BASIC/SUPERFOOD/PARENTS

This is a basic recipe for preparing rolled oats. At the second stage of eating, the oats were ground into a powder, but now baby can enjoy oatmeal without the need for the blender! Add flavor to this recipe by incorporating any of your previously frozen fruit purées and a dab of unsalted butter for wholesome goodness. Substitute whole milk for the water if you wish.

4 SERVINGS

2 cups water

1 cup old-fashioned rolled oats

1. Bring water to a boil.

2. Add oatmeal, reduce heat, and simmer, stirring occasionally, for 5–10 minutes or until water is absorbed and oats are tender.

3. Serve warm.

Soulful Grits

Note that if you want to feed grits to your baby when she's younger than ten months, you'll need to stick to instant grits, as traditional grits will be too gritty. Instead of the traditional way of cooking grits in plain water, this recipe uses chicken stock that adds a little soul to this cheesy recipe.

2 SERVINGS

¼ cup grits

1 cup low-sodium chicken stock or broth

2 tablespoons Cheddar cheese, shredded

2 tablespoons diced ham steak, cooked

1. In a small saucepan, combine grits and chicken stock or broth.

2. Bring to a boil, stirring constantly. Add cheese and ham.

3. Reduce heat, cover, and simmer for 5 minutes.

4. Serve warm.

Pinto Beans and Brown Rice

This recipe uses leftover brown rice and puréed pinto beans. Whip up a nutritious batch and pair with other Mexican favorites for a family dinner.

1 SERVING

4 tablespoons cooked brown rice

4 tablespoons Refried Pinto Beans

1. Combine brown rice and pinto bean mash.

2. If necessary, use a food processor or blender until desired consistency is reached.

Hide-and-Seek Cauliflower Mash

FREEZER/PARENTS

Here's a great game to play with your baby over mealtime: Find the cauliflower! It's buried in there somewhere!

10 SERVINGS
. . . .
2 large red-skinned potatoes, washed and chopped

1 cauliflower head, cut into florets

1 cup whole organic milk (dairy or soy)

1 tablespoon unsalted butter or olive oil

1. Place potatoes in a medium-sized pot and cover with water. Boil the potatoes for 10 minutes until soft; drain, and return to pot.

2. Steam the cauliflower until tender; drain, and add to pot with potatoes.

3. Add organic milk and unsalted butter to potatoes and cauliflower.

4. Mash with a potato masher or use a beater to get a thinner purée.

Pear–Green Bean Blend

FREEZER

Make sure to choose beans at their peak for mashing. Frozen beans are a great alternative also. Stay away from extra-large beans, which may be tough and hard to mash, and avoid beans with blemishes or bad spots altogether.

3 SERVINGS
. . . .
1 medium pear

½ cup green beans

2 cups water

1. Wash, peel, and core the pear. Cut into chunks and place in a steamer basket.

2. Wash the beans thoroughly. Trim off the ends, remove the strings, and place in the steamer basket.

3. Add enough water so that it fills the pot under the steamer basket, about 2 cups. Bring to a boil and steam for 10–15 minutes, or until beans are very soft. If the pears cook more quickly, remove them with a slotted spoon.

4. Place the beans and pears on a plate, and fork-mash them together.

Plenty of Sweets Chicken Dinner

Set aside some of the grilled chicken you make next time you're outside enjoying the beautiful weather and cooking on the grill. Use some of the previously frozen purées and you're done!

2 SERVINGS

2 ounces shredded chicken, cooked

4 tablespoons Pretty Peas (Chapter 4)

4 tablespoons Simply Sweet Potato (Chapter 4)

1. Purée chicken in a food processor or blender. Add water or broth as needed to achieve a smooth purée.

2. Combine the chicken purée with the vegetable purées.

Sautéed Spinach with Garlic

Although it may seem like a lot of spinach in the pan, the spinach will cook down. Don't add any additional oil to the pan until the spinach wilts and you can gage a little better.

4 SERVINGS

6 cups fresh spinach (baby spinach or another variety)

1 tablespoon extra-virgin olive oil

2 cloves garlic, pressed

½ tablespoon real unsalted butter

1. Wash and drain spinach well.

2. In a large skillet, heat extra-virgin olive oil over medium heat. Add garlic and unsalted butter and sauté for about 20 seconds, being careful not to burn garlic. Add spinach and cook until tender.

3. Transfer to a blender and pulse the spinach to a chunky purée or fork-mash if desired. Add water if needed. Can be frozen for up to eight weeks.

MENUS FOR TEN- TO TWELVE-MONTH-OLDS

You'll notice that your baby's eating pattern will resemble an adult eating pattern of three meals and up to three snacks per day. Remember to serve your child small healthy meals throughout the day for sustained energy, and offer portions equivalent to the size of his palm. Offer water in addition to the milk requirements, and dilute fruit juice by 50 percent or more to help prevent tooth decay.

EVERY DAY: Breast milk or whole milk (at 12 months of age): 16 ounces per day **Typical pattern:** 3 meals plus 1–3 snacks

MONDAY	TUESDAY	WEDNESDAY	THURSDAY
Strawberry and Cantaloupe Joy with yogurt	Baby Muesli with whole milk	Oatmeal with Sautéed Plantains	Good Old-Fashioned Oatmeal and 6 ounces yogurt
Tomato and Mushroom Pasta	Atlantic Cod Dinner and whole-wheat crackers	Baby's Cordon Bleu	Tofu Veg Stir-Fry
Indian Rice Pudding	Baked Zucchini	Mild Chicken and Coconut Curry Purée	Baby Ratatouille
Snack: Bread Pudding Bonanza	Snack: Baked Apples	Snack: Minted Bananas and Strawberries with organic vanilla wafers or fresh fruit	Snack: Fresh Strawberry Yogurt

FRIDAY	SATURDAY	SUNDAY	
Apples 'n' Cream	Baby Muesli	Soulful Grits	
Chicken and Spinach Stir-Fry	Captain's Fish Chowder	Plenty of Sweets Chicken Dinner	
Baby's Cordon Bleu with side of steamed broccoli	Ham and Peaches	Turkey–Sweet Potato Shepherd's Pie	
Snack: Bananas and OJ	Snack: Wild Bananas 'n' Cream	Snack: Baby's Peachy Cobbler	

CHAPTER 7

FUN AND FINGERLICIOUS FOOD (TWELVE MONTHS AND BEYOND)
Transitional Meals for Toddlers

Your baby has gone from a little explorer to an expert adventurer! From twelve months old, your toddler can have a wide array of foods, and, as a parent, you have full reign over what you can offer. The recipes in this chapter allow for self-feeding and provide your child ample practice with using eating utensils. Whole-fat cow's milk and soy milk are new additions, and the limitations on honey and citrus fruits have been lifted! Continue to make and freeze meals in advance in BPA-free containers to keep healthy meals within reach.

This chapter introduces new foods such as teething biscuits and biscotti (which can be enjoyed as early as eight months), risotto, fruit smoothies, and pizza—which all encourage self-feeding. Whole milk is an important part of your child's diet, so make sure she is getting around 16 fluid ounces per day for calcium and vitamin D. But be careful not to overdo it on the milk. Giving your child too much milk may prevent him from wanting to eat his meals. Other dairy products such as yogurt, cheese, ice cream, or milk-based smoothies will also satisfy the milk requirement.

You may continue serving all of the meals in previous chapters by dicing them instead of puréeing. If you still have frozen purées left in the freezer, use them in muffin recipes, as dips, or combine them with full-fat vanilla or plain yogurt.

FOURTH STAGE: OVER TWELVE MONTHS

Your baby has climbed all the way to the top of the developmental ladder of feeding. That little butterball is now a rambunctious toddler! Your child has now been introduced to all the food groups and should have a well-rounded palate. At this point, the golden rule for feeding toddlers is that you should incorporate five servings of fruit or vegetables into your child's diet. Your child is at a stage where she may prefer one food over another and may even express that! Therefore, in order to give your child all the nutrients his growing body needs, you may have to disguise fruit and vegetables by incorporating them into milkshakes, smoothies, pasta sauce, or baked treats. Continue to offer foods that are refused, and don't be afraid to spruce them up by adding oil, sauces, or condiments such as ketchup or mustard to them for added flavor.

The following list includes some new flavors and textures to add to your baby's diet:

- Whole cow's milk or soy milk
- Fruit smoothies and milkshakes
- Tortilla chips
- Fruit muffins (blueberry, cranberry, etc.)
- Fruity freezer pops

Keep the tooth fairy happy by limiting the amount of sugary foods your child eats. Common childhood sweets including cookies and ice cream can be made organically and healthier by adding whole, unprocessed ingredients. Keep sugary drinks at bay and only offer up to 4 ounces of 100 percent fruit juice per day to keep tooth decay away!

Sweet Potato Fries

Panko bread crumbs are Japanese bread crumbs that are more coarse than traditional store-bought crumbs. Look for it in the Asian section of your grocery or near bread crumbs and seasonings.

8 SERVINGS

4 sweet potatoes, peeled and cut into matchsticks

Large bowl of ice water

2 egg whites

⅛ teaspoon garlic powder

1 cup panko Italian-seasoned bread crumbs

1. Preheat oven to 450°F.

2. Bring a large pot of water to a boil. Place potatoes in boiling water and cook for 5 minutes. Drain and immediately plunge into bowl of ice water. Dry the potatoes well.

3. Combine egg whites and garlic powder.

4. Toss potatoes with egg white mixture, and then dip potatoes in panko bread crumbs.

5. Line baking sheet with parchment paper, place the fries on it, and bake for approximately 14 minutes.

6. Turn once, about 7 minutes into cooking.

Sweet Potato Fries 101
The moisture content of sweet potatoes is very high and often makes very soggy fries. The blanching, panko coating, and parchment paper all help to prevent soggy fries. One last tip: make sure to not crowd the baking sheet with too many potatoes. If they are too close, they steam each other and then become soggy.

Mounds of Joy Cookies

FREEZER/SUPERFOOD/PARENTS

Who doesn't love chocolate chip cookies? The nice thing about this recipe is that you can sneak in the healthy nutrition of superfoods by adding ground oats and cinnamon. The coconut makes for a chewy cookie when baked to perfection. Stand mixers are great for making cookie dough. If you have one, use it!

2 DOZEN COOKIES OR 24 SERVINGS

½ cup shortening

⅓ cup white sugar

⅓ cup brown sugar, packed

1 egg

¾ cup flour

¼ teaspoon salt

1 teaspoon baking soda

½ cup ground oats

¼ teaspoon cinnamon

¾ cup chocolate chips

3 tablespoons flaked coconut, sweetened

1. Preheat the oven to 375°F.
2. In a medium bowl, cream the shortening and sugars together. Mix with a fork until large crumbles are formed, or use an electric mixer.
3. Add the egg and mix well. Add in the flour, salt, and baking soda, continuing to stir until a dough is formed.
4. Add oatmeal, cinnamon, coconut, and chocolate chips. Stir well; then drop small spoonfuls onto a greased baking sheet, leaving about 2 inches between each cookie. Bake for 6–8 minutes.
5. Let cool on the baking sheet for 1–2 minutes; then remove and finish cooling on wire racks.

Make Them Chewylicious

Overcooking makes for a hard cookie. So when making cookies for toddlers, bake them on the soft side (rather than hard and crunchy). That means bake them just until they're done and remove them right away. Cookies that are just about done will finish cooking on the baking tray when removed from the oven, which makes a soft cookie. Don't overdo it on the baking powder or baking soda, since those ingredients tend to make cookies more cakelike.

Moist Yogurt Pancakes

SUPERFOOD/PARENTS

Serve these pancakes with fresh bananas or raspberries on top. Or, if you have any leftover frozen fruit purée, try topping these delights with it!

20 SERVINGS

1½ cups unbleached all-purpose flour

½ cup oat flour

2½ teaspoons baking powder, divided

2 teaspoons baking soda

¼ teaspoon salt

½ cup applesauce

½ cup apple juice concentrate

2 cups plain yogurt (dairy or soy)

1 teaspoon vanilla

2 tablespoons unsalted butter or trans-fat-free margarine, melted

Canola oil for pan

1. In a medium bowl, combine flours, 2 teaspoons baking powder, baking soda, and salt.

2. In a large bowl, combine applesauce with ½ teaspoon baking powder.

3. Add apple juice concentrate, yogurt, vanilla, and melted unsalted butter or trans-fat-free margarine to the applesauce mixture.

4. Slowly stir dry ingredients into wet, stirring just to combine.

5. Brush skillet or griddle with oil and heat over medium-high heat.

6. When a drop of water dances on the surface of the pan, drop batter onto surface.

7. When edges are golden and a couple of bubbles appear on the surface of the pancake, flip it and continue cooking on the other side.

8. Pancakes are ready when they are cooked through and golden on both sides.

Raspberry Strawberry Muffins

Muffins are a great way to sneak in superfoods for your baby to eat. Adding the strawberries and raspberries gives the muffin a sweet flavor. Baby won't even notice all the other healthy ingredients inside!

12 SERVINGS

2 cups white whole-wheat flour

1½ teaspoons baking powder, divided

½ teaspoon salt

½ cup applesauce

½ cup flaxseed meal

¼ cup canola oil

½ teaspoon vanilla

¾ cup maple syrup

¼ cup plain yogurt (dairy or soy)

¼ cup organic milk (dairy or soy)

¾ cup raspberries

¾ cup chopped strawberries

1. Preheat oven to 350°F.

2. In a medium bowl, combine flour, 1 teaspoon baking powder, and salt.

3. In a large bowl, combine applesauce with ½ teaspoon baking powder.

4. Add flaxseed meal, oil, vanilla, syrup, yogurt, and organic milk to the applesauce mixture. Combine well.

5. Slowly add dry ingredients to wet. Add raspberries and strawberries.

6. Spoon batter into lightly oiled muffin pan.

7. Bake 25–30 minutes, or until a toothpick inserted into the center of a muffin comes out clean.

What Is White Whole-Wheat Flour?

White whole-wheat flour is a whole-grain flour made from an albino variety of wheat. Just like the browner whole-wheat flour, white whole-wheat flour comes from all parts of the grain, so it contains the nutritional benefits of a whole grain. It provides a sweeter taste than whole-wheat flour made from the red variety of wheat, and it is usually processed into a finer flour than traditional whole-wheat flour.

Oat-Cran Cookies

This recipe adds a touch of cranberries, a powerhouse food filled with antioxidants, to these chewy cookies. If you're really ambitious, you can add a zest of orange to add a hint of citrus flavor.

5 SERVINGS

½ cup shortening

¼ cup white sugar

½ cup brown sugar, packed

1 egg

½ teaspoon vanilla

½ cup flour

⅛ teaspoon cinnamon

¼ teaspoon salt

½ teaspoon baking soda

1½ cups rolled oats (quick or old-fashioned)

⅓ cup dried cranberries

1. Preheat the oven to 350°F.

2. In a medium bowl, cream the shortening and white and brown sugar together (mix with a fork until large crumbles are formed, or use an electric mixer).

3. Add the egg and vanilla, mixing well. Add in the flour, cinnamon, salt, and baking soda, continuing to stir until a dough is formed.

4. Add in the oatmeal and cranberries. Stir well; then drop spoonfuls onto a greased baking sheet, leaving about 2 inches in between each cookie. Bake for 9–11 minutes.

5. Let cool on the baking sheet for 1–2 minutes; then remove and finish cooling on wire racks.

Freeze That Dough

Make batches of cookie dough ahead of time and freeze the dough for up to twelve weeks. Freeze the dough in small batches, enough to make 8–10 cookies. This is a great way to keep homemade cookie dough on hand and is also easy on your wallet.

Mika's Rainbow Corn Medley

Every member of your family will thoroughly enjoy this recipe because it's colorful and packed with lots of sweet and savory flavors.

8 SERVINGS

3 tablespoons extra-virgin olive oil

4 cups frozen corn kernels

¼ cup red pepper, diced

¼ cup orange pepper, diced

¼ cup yellow pepper, diced

¼ cup green pepper, diced

Dab of unsalted butter

¼ teaspoon garlic salt

2 tablespoons organic flour

½ cup chopped parsley

¼ cup grated Parmesan cheese

1. Heat oil over medium-high heat in a skillet.

2. Add corn and peppers. Sauté for about 10 minutes or until corn is heated through.

3. Add a dab of butter, garlic salt to taste, flour, and parsley. Sauté for 5 minutes more.

4. Top with grated Parmesan cheese. Serve warm.

Broccoli and Cheese Balls

FREEZER/SUPERFOOD/PARENTS

Skip the drive-through and serve up this healthy meat-free alternative to fast-food chicken nuggets. Save time by making these in advance using fresh broccoli and freezing them for later.

3 SERVINGS

¾ cup frozen broccoli

2 cups water

½ cup mozzarella cheese

1 large egg

¼ cup plain bread crumbs

2 tablespoons canola oil

1. Wash the broccoli and dice into small pieces. Cover with water in a saucepan and bring to a boil. Cook for 15 minutes, or until the broccoli is tender. Drain and let cool; then either purée in a food processor or fork-mash.

2. Grate the mozzarella, and mix it with the cooked mashed broccoli. Pour in a beaten egg and mix thoroughly to combine.

3. Tightly mold a small ball of broccoli and cheese with your hands. Roll it in bread crumbs to cover on all sides, and place on a plate. Repeat until all the balls are made.

4. Heat the oil in a frying pan. When hot, carefully place the broccoli cheese balls into the pan. Fry for 1–2 minutes; turn over with a spatula. Let fry for another 1–2 minutes; turn over again. Nuggets are cooked when all sides are lightly browned.

5. Drain onto paper towels. Serve as finger food once cooled.

Cheesy Corn Nuggets

SUPERFOOD/PARENTS

When made with buttermilk and cornmeal, these fried babies are also called hushpuppies in Southern states.

4 SERVINGS

1 cup canned corn or 3 ears cooked fresh corn

1 egg

2 tablespoons flour

½ tablespoon melted unsalted butter

¼ cup shredded Cheddar cheese

2 tablespoons canola oil

1. Shave the corn off the sides of ears of cooked corn, yielding 1 cup of corn kernels. Mash it well with a fork or run it through the food processor.

2. Whisk the egg in a medium bowl. Add the flour, melted butter, shredded cheese, and corn, mixing thoroughly to combine.

3. Heat the oil in a frying pan. When hot, drop the batter into the pan by the spoonful, leaving enough space between them so that the fritters do not touch.

4. Let fry 2–3 minutes; then flip over with a spatula. Cook another 2–3 minutes, flipping again if necessary.

5. Drain onto paper towels. Serve as finger food once cooled.

Sautéed Sugar Snap Peas and Pearls

FREEZER/PARENTS

Pearl onions offer a mild flavor suitable for toddlers. Other mild onions include the yellow Bermuda onion, the white Spanish onion, and the red Italian onion. Feel free to use any of these but cut back the amount if the onion flavor seems too strong.

1 SERVING

¼ cup pearl onions, peeled

1 tablespoon unsalted butter

¼ cup sugar snap peas

½ cup water

1. Cut each pearl onion into quarters.

2. Melt the butter in a deep frying pan; then add the onions. Cook over medium heat for several minutes, stirring constantly to prevent burning or sticking.

3. If using fresh pea pods, select ones that are firm, bright green, and medium size. Snap off the ends, and remove the strings from each pea. Or substitute frozen sugar snap peas.

4. Add the water and peas into the frying pan. Bring to a boil; then simmer for 10–15 minutes, or until peas are cooked and tender.

5. Allow to cool, then either serve as is or fork-mash if desired.

Pearl Onions

As the name suggests, pearl onions are very small, round, white onions. They're typically ½"–1" in diameter and are the primary onion used in making pickled onions. They're good for introducing onions to toddlers because they're relatively mild and sweet.

Homemade Biter Biscuits

BASIC/SUPERFOOD

Why settle for store-bought teething biscuits when you get make your own organic version? Keep these on hand when your baby wants something to chew on. The end result should be hard and crunchy. If it crumbles and breaks, it's too soft for baby.

20 SERVINGS

⅔ cup milk or water

4 tablespoons unsalted butter, melted and cooled, or canola oil

1 tablespoon brown sugar

1 cup wheat germ (toasted or untoasted)

1 cup whole-wheat flour

1. Beat together milk or water, unsalted butter or oil, and sugar.

2. Stir in wheat germ and flour, and knead for 8–10 minutes until dough is smooth and satiny. Add more water or more flour if necessary.

3. Make small balls of dough and roll them into sticks that are about ½-inch thick and 4 inches long.

4. Roll out on floured surface to a ½-inch thickness.

5. Bake on a greased cookie sheet at 350°F for 45 minutes, or until the biscuits are hard and browned.

Teething Biscuit Safety

Wait until your baby comfortably eats solid puréed foods before offering her a teething biscuit. Always supervise your baby carefully while she's eating one—ideally she'll gnaw on the hard biscuit, getting relief for her sore gums while eating some of it, very slowly, in the process. It's always possible that she could break off a piece big enough to choke on, so be careful.

Baby Biscotti

BASIC/SUPERFOOD

While you may like biscotti dipped in chocolate or nuts to go with your coffee, your baby will appreciate this hard yet comforting delight to smash against her gums.

8–10 SERVINGS

1 cup all-purpose flour

2 tablespoons brown sugar

½ teaspoon baking powder

¼ teaspoon baking soda

1 egg yolk

1 tablespoon oil

⅓ cup milk, water, or soy milk

1. Mix together flour, sugar, baking powder, and baking soda.

2. Add egg yolk, oil, and milk. Stir until the mixture forms a firm dough.

3. Shape the dough into a log about 6 inches long. Place on a greased cookie sheet, and press the log into a bar about 2 inches wide. Bake at 325°F for 20 minutes; then cool until the log is cool enough to touch.

4. Cut diagonally into ½-inch slices. Spread out on the cookie sheet; then bake for another 10–15 minutes. Slices should be crispy and dry.

5. Cool on wire racks.

Quick Teething Rusks

BASIC/SUPERFOOD

Rusks, usually called cookies in North America, are a type of hard biscuit perfect for teething because they absorb the saliva from baby's mouth. That means less of it getting on you!

8 SERVINGS

¼ cup unsalted butter or margarine

1 cup self-rising flour

1 egg yolk

¼ cup milk, water, or soy milk

1. Preheat oven to 375°F. Combine the unsalted butter into the flour with a fork. Mix together until coarse crumbs are formed.

2. Add in the egg yolk and milk. Stir until it forms a smooth dough, adding more or less liquid as necessary.

3. Roll the dough to a 1-inch thickness on a lightly floured surface. Cut into 1-inch slices and place on a greased cookie sheet.

4. Bake at 375°F for 20–25 minutes, or until browned. Cool on a wire rack.

Other Ways to Crisp a Biscuit

Cooking baby biscuits is more of an art than a science. While it's easiest to bake them all in one go, you can shorten the cooking time by "flash cooking" at a higher temperature for the first 10–15 minutes. You'll want to lower the temperature after that, though, to avoid burning before the biscuits are thoroughly cooked.

Cheesy Polenta with Roasted Vegetables

FREEZER/SUPERFOOD/PARENTS

The taste of Italy shines through this creamy polenta dish. Polenta comes from boiled cornmeal and is an important component of northern Italian cooking.

8 TO 10 SERVINGS

2 carrots

4 asparagus spears

6 mushrooms (button or cremini)

2 tablespoons extra-virgin olive oil

⅛ teaspoon salt

3 cups water

1 cup polenta

½ cup Cheddar cheese (dairy or soy)

1. Preheat oven to 425°F.

2. Peel carrots and cut into ¼-inch-wide matchsticks.

3. Break off tough ends of asparagus, and cut into 1-inch-long pieces.

4. Cut mushrooms in half.

5. Toss vegetables in extra-virgin olive oil and salt. Spread on baking sheet and cook until tender, approximately 10–15 minutes.

6. While vegetables are cooking, bring water to a boil in a medium saucepan.

7. Slowly whisk in polenta and keep whisking until polenta thickens and pulls away from the sides of the pan.

8. Sprinkle on cheese, and stir to melt.

9. In a large bowl, stir to combine polenta and vegetables.

Stuffed Pepper Surprise

If you're already outside with your friends for a barbecue, instead of turning on the hot oven, pop these peppers right on the grill. Put them on once the heat dies down and let them cook under the cover until the pepper turns soft to the touch.

2 SERVINGS

1 large bell pepper

¼ pound ground beef

¼ cup cooked white or brown rice

¼ cup tomato sauce

1 ounce cheese, shredded

Dash of salt and pepper

1. Preheat the oven to 350°F.

2. Wash the pepper and cut off the top. Remove all seeds from the cavity.

3. Brown the ground beef in a skillet over medium heat for 10 minutes, or until it's completely cooked. Drain any fat and return beef to the pan.

4. Mix the rice, tomato sauce, cheese, salt, and pepper in with the beef. Continue cooking over low heat for 3–4 minutes, or until the cheese is melted.

5. Place the bell pepper in a deep baking dish. Pour the meat mixture inside; then bake for 1 hour, or until the green pepper is tender.

Other Pepper Fillings

Bell peppers can be stuffed with a variety of fillings. If baby doesn't like meat, try stuffing these with rice, cheese, and tomatoes instead. Or, for a Southwestern twist, make a filling with corn, onions, tomatoes, and a dash of chili powder.

Mini Pizza Faces

FREEZER/SUPERFOOD/PARENTS

English muffins make instant pizza crust! Most kids love pizza, so this dish is sure to put a smile on everyone's faces.

2 SERVINGS

1 baby carrot

2 tablespoons peas

2 cups water

1 English muffin

2 tablespoons tomato sauce

4 thin slices pepperoni

1 ounce shredded mozzarella

1. Preheat the oven to 375°F.

2. Slice the baby carrot in half lengthwise. Place it and the peas in a saucepan with the water. Bring to a boil; then cook for about 10 minutes, or until the vegetables are tender. Drain and set aside.

3. Split the English muffin in half and lay the two pieces face-up on a baking sheet. Spoon tomato sauce over each muffin to cover it and lay a foundation for the pizza face.

4. On each muffin, place 2 pieces of pepperoni for eyes. Place half a baby carrot for a nose. Make a smile out of peas. Place the shredded mozzarella around the top of the muffin for hair.

5. Bake for 10–15 minutes, or until the cheese melts.

Easy Kid-Friendly Pizza Sauce
Combine 1 can tomato paste, ½ teaspoon garlic powder, ½ teaspoon oregano, ½ teaspoon basil, and ¾ teaspoon agave nectar for a tasty, easy pizza sauce. Store extra sauce in an airtight container in the refrigerator.

Grandma's Meat Biscuit Roll

This innovative dish makes a great entrée for the whole family. Feel free to make plenty more, especially save some for Grandma!

4 SERVINGS
. . . .

½ pound ground beef

2 tablespoons tomato sauce

1 teaspoon parsley

1 teaspoon oregano

2 cups pastry flour

3 teaspoons baking powder

¼ teaspoon salt

¼ cup shortening

½ cup cold milk or water

1. Preheat the oven to 350°F. Brown the ground beef in a skillet until the meat is completely cooked, about 10–15 minutes. Drain the fat.

2. Mix in the tomato sauce, parsley, and oregano. Stir well; simmer over low heat for another 5 minutes.

3. Sift the flour with the baking powder and salt (be sure there are no lumps of baking powder, or someone will be getting a rather unpleasant bite). Work in the shortening with a fork until it forms large crumbles. Add in the cold milk, 1 tablespoon at a time, and stir until a thick batter is formed. If the dough is too sticky, add more flour.

4. Roll out the dough on a floured work surface. Place the cooked meat into the middle and roll the dough up so that it folds over to make a cylinder. Place on a greased baking sheet.

5. Bake for 30 minutes, or until the biscuit is golden brown. Cut into slices before serving.

Blueberry Mini Muffins

You can also use frozen blueberries for this recipe. If you are using frozen, the batter will take on a purple hue unless you thaw them first.

42 MINI MUFFINS; 21 SERVINGS

2 cups white whole-wheat flour

1½ teaspoons baking powder, divided

½ teaspoon salt

½ cup applesauce

½ cup flaxseed meal

¼ cup canola oil

½ teaspoon vanilla

¾ cup apple juice concentrate

¼ cup plain yogurt (dairy or soy)

¼ cup organic milk (dairy or soy)

1½ cups fresh blueberries

1. Preheat oven to 350°F.
2. In a medium bowl, combine flour, 1 teaspoon baking powder, and salt.
3. In a large bowl, combine applesauce with ½ teaspoon baking powder.
4. Add flaxseed meal, oil, vanilla, apple juice concentrate, yogurt, and organic milk. Combine well.
5. Slowly add dry ingredients to wet. Add blueberries.
6. Spoon batter into lightly oiled mini muffin pan.
7. Bake 25–30 minutes, or until a toothpick inserted into the center of a muffin comes out clean.

All-Mighty Flaxseed

Flaxseed is a great source of omega-3 fatty acids and a good source of dietary fiber. Although flaxseed is available whole or ground, it is believed that ground flaxseed provides the better source of nutrition. In addition to incorporating this nutritional powerhouse into baked goods, ground flaxseed can also be sprinkled on cereal or yogurt.

Chicken and Dumplings

This comforting classic takes a while to prepare, but it's well worth it in the long run! The best part about it—it's all organic! Make up a big batch and freeze the rest for later.

4 SERVINGS

1 drumstick or thigh piece of chicken

6 cups water

1 small russet potato, diced

1 medium carrot, diced

Dash of salt and pepper

⅛ teaspoon dill

1 egg

1 cup all-purpose flour

¼ cup water

1 cup chicken broth

1. Wash the chicken well, and remove the skin if desired. Bring to a boil in 6 cups water. Simmer for 1–1½ hours, or until the meat begins falling off the bone.

2. Remove the meat from the pot. Take off all the fat, skin, and bones. Shred the chicken into small pieces; then add back to the pot.

3. Add potatoes and carrots to the chicken pot, along with the salt, pepper, and dill. Simmer for 30–40 minutes, or until the vegetables are tender.

4. Lightly beat the egg; add in the flour. Stir well; then add water 1 tablespoon at a time until a stiff dough is formed. Roll out the dough; then cut into small strips.

5. Bring the chicken pot back to a boil. Add in the dumplings and broth; then simmer for an additional 40–45 minutes.

Making It Creamy

If your family prefers their stews on the creamy side (and no one has an intolerance or allergy to dairy products), you can add a cup of heavy cream or half-and-half instead of the broth to the stew during the last hour of simmering. In terms of just thickening the stew, adding dumplings should do the job.

Broccoli a la Pasta

Don't hold back on the garlic in this recipe! Use as much as you want. It adds a wonderful flavor when it combines with the olive oil. Serve this dish for the whole family.

2 SERVINGS

½ cup broccoli

4 cups chicken or vegetable stock

1 cup farfalle pasta

1 teaspoon extra-virgin olive oil

½ clove garlic, minced

1 teaspoon parsley

1 teaspoon grated Parmesan cheese

1. Wash the broccoli and dice into small florets.

2. Bring the stock to a boil. Add the pasta and cook for about 10 minutes. Add in the broccoli and cook for another 10 minutes, or until both pasta and broccoli are tender. When cooked, drain.

3. Heat the extra-virgin olive oil in a medium skillet. Add garlic and parsley, sautéing for 2–3 minutes.

4. Add the pasta and broccoli to the saucepan. Sauté for 2–3 minutes, tossing the pasta and broccoli together with the garlic.

5. Sprinkle with Parmesan cheese before serving.

Other Types of Pastas
At many well-stocked grocery stores, a variety of pastas are made from organic grains. These options run the gamut from the traditional semolina to whole wheat, quinoa, corn, and rice. Try them with tomato-based sauces, in soups, or tossed with olive oil and Parmesan cheese.

Banana Bread

FREEZER/SUPERFOOD/PARENTS

When you have ripe bananas with brown spots on the skin, their soft and sweet flavor is perfect for banana bread. This is a perfect recipe to make in the fall to wind down from the summer and bring warmth into your home.

1 LOAF; 24 SERVINGS

2 cups white whole-wheat flour

1 tablespoon plus ½ teaspoon baking powder, divided

1 teaspoon baking soda

¾ teaspoon salt

½ cup applesauce

½ cup unsalted butter or trans-fat-free margarine, softened

2 tablespoons apple juice concentrate

⅓ cup agave nectar

1 teaspoon vanilla

4 ripe bananas

1. Preheat oven to 350°F.

2. In a medium bowl combine flour, 1 tablespoon baking powder, baking soda, and salt.

3. In a large bowl, combine applesauce with ½ teaspoon baking powder.

4. Thoroughly mix in butter or margarine, apple juice concentrate, agave nectar, and vanilla.

5. Mash bananas.

6. Mix bananas into wet ingredients.

7. Slowly mix dry ingredients into wet.

8. Pour batter into a lightly oiled standard loaf pan.

9. Bake 1 hour or until a toothpick inserted into the center of the loaf comes out clean.

10. Cool 10 minutes in pan; then cool completely on cooling rack.

Limit Salt and Sugar

Since babies don't have preconceived notions about how specific foods are supposed to taste, let them taste the purity of the high-quality organic ingredients you are using. Babies don't expect foods to be salty or sweet, so if they aren't introduced to excessive salt and sugar, they can develop the good habit of liking food the way nature intended it to taste.

Sweet-and-Sour Meatballs

Sweet-and-sour sauce offers a balance between the two flavors. Some toddlers really like it and some could do without it. Use ketchup or grape preserves for dipping, and make the meatballs plain if your child isn't a fan.

2 SERVINGS

¼ pound ground beef

¼ cup bread crumbs

½ teaspoon soy sauce

2 teaspoons oil

¼ cup bell pepper, diced

½ cup canned pineapple chunks, diced; reserve juice

1 teaspoon cornstarch

2 tablespoons water

1. Mix the ground beef, bread crumbs, and soy sauce together. Form into round 1-inch balls.

2. Heat the oil in a skillet. Add the meatballs, reduce heat to medium, and cook until the meatballs are no longer pink.

3. Wash the bell pepper and dice into small pieces. Dice the pineapple chunks into small pieces.

4. Put the pineapple chunks and juice into a small bowl. Add cornstarch and water, and stir well to mix. Add in the bell pepper.

5. Pour the pineapple mixture into the skillet. Stir the meatballs around to coat in the sauce, and cook the sauce for several minutes or until it thickens.

6. Allow to cool before serving.

Let's Stay Together

If your meatballs fall apart when you cook on the stovetop, try adding a little oil to the pan to keep them from sticking and falling apart when you roll them over. Also, adding more egg and bread crumbs (and pressing the meat very firmly into balls) will keep them from disintegrating into meat sauce.

Happy Birthday Vanilla Cake

Try this healthier birthday cake for your child's first birthday. It uses apple juice and maple syrup for sweetness instead of refined sugar. Top with whipped cream and fresh berries instead of frosting if you're going the healthier route.

15–22 SERVINGS

1 cup white, all-purpose flour

½ cup oat flour

2¼ teaspoons baking powder, divided

¼ teaspoon salt

¼ cup applesauce

½ cup apple juice concentrate

½ cup organic milk (dairy or soy)

¼ cup canola oil

¼ cup maple syrup

1½ teaspoons vanilla

1. Preheat oven to 375°F.

2. Lightly oil an 8" or 9" square or round cake pan.

3. In a medium mixing bowl, combine flours, 2 teaspoons baking powder, and salt.

4. In a large mixing bowl, combine applesauce with ¼ teaspoon baking powder.

5. Add apple juice concentrate, organic milk, oil, syrup, and vanilla to the applesauce.

6. Mix dry ingredients into wet, one half at a time.

7. Scrape batter into pan.

8. Bake 25 minutes, or until a toothpick inserted into the middle comes out clean.

Homemade Oat Flour

Make your own oat flour by taking old-fashioned rolled oats and blending them in the blender or food processor. Keep blending until you have a fine, powdery flour. Replacing a portion of white flour with oat flour will provide some whole-grain goodness to your dessert recipes.

Broccoli with Meat and Rigatoni

FREEZER/SUPERFOOD/PARENTS

For a vegetarian dish, try this with protein crumbles as a meat substitute.

16 SERVINGS

1 pound whole-wheat rigatoni pasta
½ pound ground beef
3 tablespoons extra-virgin olive oil
1 tablespoon unsalted butter
4 garlic cloves, minced
1 bunch broccoli separated into florets
1 cup free-range chicken or beef broth
1 cup fresh basil, coarsely chopped, divided
Fresh parsley, chopped
Parmesan cheese

1. Cook rigatoni pasta according to directions, drain, and set aside.

2. In medium pan, brown ground beef. Drain and set aside.

3. In a large skillet, heat 3 tablespoons olive oil and butter. Sauté garlic until browned over medium heat. Add broccoli and stir gently until coated.

4. Add chicken broth and simmer until broccoli is al dente. (Al dente means that it is still slightly firm. This amount of broccoli should take about 8 minutes to become al dente.)

5. Add half the basil, drained rigatoni, and ground beef to skillet and mix thoroughly.

6. Transfer to serving bowl, top with remaining basil, parsley, and Parmesan cheese.

Whole-Wheat Mac 'n' Cheese

For an interesting twist, try different kinds of pasta or pasta shapes such as shells, rigatoni, farfalle, penne, or ziti.

20 SERVINGS

10 cups water

½ pound whole-wheat elbow macaroni

6 tablespoons unsalted butter

6 tablespoons all-purpose flour

3 cups 2% organic milk

1 cup grated organic mild Cheddar cheese

½ cup grated sharp organic Cheddar cheese

½ cup grated Colby cheese

½ teaspoon salt

½ teaspoon pepper

½ cup diced tomatoes

1. In a large pot, boil the 10 cups water. Add whole-wheat elbow macaroni and cook until tender. Drain and rinse well under cold running water.

2. In a large saucepan over medium heat, melt unsalted butter. Add flour and continue stirring until the mixture thickens.

3. Add organic milk and continue to stir until this thickens up.

4. Remove from heat and add cheeses, salt, pepper, and tomatoes. If needed, return to low heat and stir to melt cheese.

5. Add cooked elbow macaroni and mix well. Serve.

Zucchini Corn Muffins

Most toddlers won't eat a whole corn muffin. Cut the muffin in half and enjoy the other half for yourself. Tastes great with Puréed Collard Greens (Chapter 5).

12 MUFFINS; 24 SERVINGS

1 cup cornmeal

1 cup white whole-wheat flour

2¼ teaspoons baking powder, divided

1 teaspoon baking soda

½ teaspoon salt

¼ cup applesauce

½ cup apple juice concentrate

¾ cup organic milk (dairy or soy)

3 tablespoons melted unsalted butter or trans-fat-free margarine

1 cup grated zucchini

1. Preheat oven to 400°F.

2. In a medium bowl, combine cornmeal, flour, 2 teaspoons baking powder, baking soda, and salt.

3. In a large bowl, combine applesauce with ¼ teaspoon baking powder.

4. Add apple juice concentrate, organic milk, and butter or trans-fat-free margarine to the applesauce.

5. Slowly mix dry ingredients into wet.

6. Mix in zucchini.

7. Spoon into oiled muffin pan.

8. Bake 18–22 minutes, or until a toothpick inserted into the center of a muffin comes out clean.

Blueberry Pancakes

FREEZER/SUPERFOOD/PARENTS

There's nothing like the aroma of homemade blueberry pancakes with warm maple syrup and the smell of bacon or sausage floating throughout the rooms on a beautiful fall morning.

15 SERVINGS

1 cup whole-wheat pastry flour

2 tablespoons brown sugar

2 tablespoons baking powder

¼ teaspoon salt

1 tablespoon flaxseed meal

1½ cups old-fashioned oats

2 cups buttermilk

3 eggs, beaten

¼ cup canola oil

1 pint fresh blueberries

1. Lightly oil a griddle and preheat to low-medium heat.

2. In large bowl, mix pastry flour, brown sugar, baking powder, salt, and flaxseed meal.

3. In separate bowl, mix old-fashioned oats and buttermilk. Then add beaten eggs and canola oil with a whisk until smooth and well blended.

4. Mix wet and dry ingredients together. Fold in blueberries.

5. Pour ¼ cup batter at a time onto the hot griddle. Cook until bubbles are seen and then flip.

Pumpkin Risotto

This colorful dish makes a lovely presentation when served with a Cornish hen and a side of asparagus, or for baby, serve it alongside the Rosemary Cornish Hen Dinner (Chapter 5). A great way to welcome winter.

10 SERVINGS

1 tablespoon extra-virgin olive oil

1 tablespoon unsalted butter or trans-fat-free margarine

1 tablespoon fresh sage

1 garlic clove, minced

¼ cup chopped onion

1 cup arborio rice

1 cup canned pumpkin

3 cups vegetable broth

1. Preheat oven to 350°F.

2. In a small skillet, heat extra-virgin olive oil and unsalted butter or trans-fat-free margarine over medium-high heat.

3. When oil mixture is sizzling, add sage and minced garlic. Sauté for 1 minute.

4. Transfer herb mixture to a 3-quart casserole.

5. Add remaining ingredients and cover.

6. Bake 1 hour. Stir before serving.

Pumpkin Varieties

There are many different varieties of pumpkins—and the ones you carve on Halloween won't taste particularly good! Look for the ones called "cooking pumpkins," "pie pumpkins," or some other designation that indicates they are meant to be eaten, not carved.

Under the Sea Fish Sticks

SUPERFOOD

Skip the freezer aisle and make your own fish sticks with organic ingredients. Cod works great for making fish sticks because you don't have to worry about picking out the bones, although it doesn't hurt to double-check.

1 SERVING

1 Atlantic cod fillet

1 large egg

½ cup milk

¼ cup flour

¼ cup plain bread crumbs

1. Preheat oven to 400°F. Grease a baking sheet or oven-proof dish.

2. Rinse the fish fillet and remove all bones. Cut into slices.

3. Beat the egg and milk together in a small bowl. Place the flour in a pile on one small plate, and the bread crumbs in a pile on another small plate.

4. Dip each fish stick into flour, then egg, then bread crumbs. Shake gently to remove any excess and place on the baking sheet.

5. Bake for 15–18 minutes. Flip the fish sticks over halfway during cooking. Cool before serving as finger food.

Plantation Chicken

PARENTS

Many Caribbean cultures cook with plantains on a regular basis. Unlike bananas, plantains must be cooked and not eaten raw. This simple recipe allows your toddler to discover new flavors from the Caribbean.

2 SERVINGS

1 small boneless skinless chicken breast (about 6 ounces)

2 tablespoons melted unsalted butter

1 plantain

Dash of cinnamon

1. Preheat the oven to 350°F. Wash the chicken breast and remove any skin or fat.

2. Brush both sides of the breast with butter. Place in a greased ovenproof dish.

3. Cut the ends off of the plantain with a knife. Peel the plantain from the skin. Cut into thin slices and place on top of the chicken. Drizzle the remaining melted unsalted butter on top of the plantain. Top with a dash of cinnamon.

4. Heat the oven to 350°F. Bake for 30 minutes or until the chicken's internal temperature reaches 170°F. The juice from the chicken should run clear when pricked with a fork.

5. Allow to cool; then cut into small pieces and serve. You can also fork-mash if desired.

Pineapply Salsa

Instead of just adding the pineapple into this salsa, how about grilling it first? Cut fresh pineapple into ½-inch thick slices. Place on medium-hot grill and grill for 5–7 minutes per side. Cool for about 10 minutes or so before adding to dish.

12 SERVINGS

1 cup diced fresh pineapple

½ cup red bell pepper, diced

½ cup yellow bell pepper, diced

½ cup black beans, drained and rinsed

¼ cup red onion, diced

¼ cup cilantro, finely chopped

¼ cup orange-pineapple juice

2 tablespoons lime juice

Salt and pepper to taste

1. In a large bowl, combine pineapple, red and yellow peppers, black beans, red onion, and cilantro and mix well.

2. In a small bowl, combine orange-pineapple juice and lime juice. Pour into large bowl.

3. Mix all ingredients together, and season with salt and pepper to taste.

Chicken with Apricots

Allow your baby to feed herself. You can offer a fork for practice, but her fingers will work perfectly.

2 SERVINGS
. . . .

1 small boneless skinless chicken breast
(about 6 ounces)

1 ripe apricot

1 tablespoon apricot preserves

½ tablespoon unsalted butter

1. Wash the chicken breast and remove any skin or fat. Place in the bottom of a greased ovenproof baking dish.

2. Dice the apricot into small pieces. Mix with the apricot preserves; then spread over the chicken.

3. Dot the top of the chicken with unsalted butter; then bake at 350°F for 30 minutes or until the chicken's internal temperature reaches 170°F. The juice from the chicken should run clear when pricked with a fork, and the chicken meat should not be pink when sliced.

4. Allow to cool; then dice into small pieces for baby to self-feed. You can also fork-mash if desired.

Spiced Pumpkin Muffins

During the autumn months, purchase a big pumpkin and go on a cooking spree. Invite your friends' kids over and see how many baked treats you can make out of the one pumpkin, including this one. Then, give the goods away as gifts!

12 SERVINGS

2½ cups white whole-wheat flour

2¼ teaspoons baking powder, divided

¾ teaspoon salt

1½ teaspoons cinnamon

½ teaspoon nutmeg

¾ cup applesauce

¼ cup canola oil

¼ cup blackstrap molasses

½ cup agave nectar

1 teaspoon vanilla

2 cups cooked pumpkin (or 1 15-ounce can)

1. Preheat oven to 350°F.
2. In a medium bowl, combine flour, 1½ teaspoons baking powder, salt, cinnamon, and nutmeg.
3. In a large bowl, combine applesauce with remaining ¾ teaspoon baking powder.
4. Add oil, molasses, agave nectar, vanilla, and pumpkin to applesauce mixture. Stir to combine.
5. Slowly add dry ingredients to wet.
6. Spoon into oiled muffin pan.
7. Bake 25–30 minutes, or until a toothpick inserted into the center of a muffin comes out clean.

What Is Blackstrap Molasses?

Blackstrap molasses is a byproduct of the process that converts sugar cane into table sugar. It is the byproduct of the third boiling. Molasses from other stages of the sugar production process are available as well; however, they don't have the same nutritional makeup as blackstrap molasses. Blackstrap molasses is a good source of calcium, copper, potassium, and manganese. It is also a rich sweetener that adds depth to baked beans, barbecue sauce, and gingerbread.

Tuna Fishcakes

Fish stock can be found in the aisle with all the stocks at the grocery store. It will add extra flavor to this dish, but it is still good without it. Substitute a boneless fillet of orange roughy or cod for tuna.

2 SERVINGS

1 boneless tuna fillet (3–4 ounces)
1 medium red potato
2 cups water or fish stock
1 egg
1 teaspoon parsley
½ cup bread crumbs
1 tablespoon extra-virgin olive oil

1. Rinse the fish fillet and remove all bones. Cut into small pieces.

2. Wash and peel the potato; then dice into small pieces.

3. Bring the water to a boil in a medium saucepan. Add the fish and potato; then cook for 20–25 minutes, or until the fish is cooked and the potato is tender.

4. Fork-mash the fish and potato in a small bowl. Add the egg and parsley, then mix thoroughly. Form into patties. Put the bread crumbs on plate, and roll each patty in bread crumbs so that it's well coated.

5. Heat the oil in a nonstick skillet. Sauté the patties 2–3 minutes, or until lightly browned; then flip and repeat on the other side. Drain on paper towels before serving.

Breakfast Pizza

Coat the bananas in orange or lemon juice right away to prevent from browning due to the enzyme in them that reacts with oxygen. The acidic juices from oranges and lemons prevent the browning process.

4 SERVINGS

1 large whole-wheat tortilla

½ teaspoon unsalted butter or trans-fat-free light spread

1 teaspoon table sugar

⅛ teaspoon cinnamon

⅓ cup organic whipped cream cheese (dairy or soy)

2 teaspoons honey

¼ **cup blueberries**

¼ **cup strawberries, sliced**

½ cup blackberries

¼ cup bananas, sliced

¼ cup kiwi, diced

1. Preheat oven to 400°F.

2. Place whole-wheat tortilla on an ungreased cookie sheet.

3. Spread unsalted butter evenly over tortilla.

4. In a small bowl, combine table sugar and cinnamon. Sprinkle this over the top of the tortilla.

5. Bake tortilla for 3–4 minutes or until edges begin to brown. Remove from oven.

6. In a medium bowl, beat cream cheese with honey until well mixed.

7. Spread over the tortilla, forming a base for the fruit toppings.

8. Arrange fruit on top of tortilla. Cut into pizza slices and serve.

Fluffy Lemon Pudding

SUPERFOOD/PARENTS

Stir in strawberries, raspberries, or blueberries in this pudding for an even tastier treat.

4 SERVINGS

1 egg, separated

½ cup sugar

2 tablespoons all-purpose flour

Dash salt

2 teaspoons lemon zest

3 tablespoons lemon juice

½ cup milk (regular or soy)

1. Preheat oven to 350°F.

2. Place the egg yolk in a bowl. Beat in the sugar. Add in the flour, salt, and lemon zest. Stir in lemon juice and milk, and mix well.

3. In a separate bowl, whip the egg white to soft peaks using an electric mixer. Beat on high until the egg whites form small white peaks when you lift one of the beaters out of the bowl. Fold the egg white into the rest of the batter.

4. Pour into a baking dish. Bake for 45 minutes, or until the pudding is set.

5. Let cool before serving, though adults may prefer the pudding warm. Store leftovers in the refrigerator.

Pear Pudding

This unique homemade pudding makes a nice snack that the entire family will enjoy!

2 SERVINGS
. . . .

1 medium pear

1 egg, separated

1 teaspoon lemon zest

½ teaspoon cinnamon

2 tablespoons sugar

3 tablespoons all-purpose flour

2 tablespoons milk (regular or soy)

1. Preheat the oven to 375°F. Wash and peel the pear. Remove the stem and seeds, and grate the pear flesh.

2. Place the egg yolk in a bowl. Beat in lemon zest, cinnamon, and sugar. Mix in flour and milk; then stir in grated pear.

3. Whip the egg white to soft peaks using an electric mixer. Beat on high until, when you lift one of the beaters out of the bowl, the egg whites form small white peaks. Fold the egg white into the pear mixture.

4. Pour into a greased baking dish. Bake for about 30 minutes, or until pudding is set.

5. Allow to cool before serving.

Cheese Quesadillas with Tomato and Avocado

SUPERFOOD/PARENTS

To add more protein to this recipe, add beans or meat such as chicken or beef.

4 SERVINGS

1 ripe avocado

2 whole-wheat tortillas

1 ripe tomato

¼ cup organic shredded Cheddar cheese (dairy or soy)

1 teaspoon canola oil

Mild salsa for garnish

1. Cut avocado, remove pit, and scrape out the insides. Mash avocado flesh with a fork.

2. Add avocado mash on top of 1 tortilla.

3. Dice tomato and layer on top of avocado.

4. Sprinkle cheese on top of this layer and top with second tortilla.

5. In medium skillet, heat canola oil. Place quesadilla in skillet. Heat until cheese begins to melt. Flip and cook to golden brown. Remove from heat and cut into eight triangles.

6. Top with mild salsa.

Baked Chicken Nuggets

FREEZER/PARENTS

There's no need to rely on the fried version of this kids' favorite when it's this easy to make your own healthier baked version. Your kids will ask for more!

2 SERVINGS

1 small boneless skinless chicken breast (about 6 ounces), trimmed of fat

1 cup bread crumbs or corn flakes

¼ teaspoon fresh or dried parsley

½ teaspoon garlic powder

¼ teaspoon onion powder

1. Cut chicken into bite-sized pieces.

2. If using corn flakes, crush into a fine powder. Add the parsley, garlic powder, and onion powder to bread crumbs or crushed corn flakes, and mix well.

3. Roll chicken in the flakes or bread crumbs; set aside.

4. Preheat the oven to 400°F. Place the breaded nuggets on a greased baking sheet and cook for about 15 minutes, or until the chicken is white when you slice into it.

5. Drain any residual grease onto paper towels, and serve once cooled.

Roasted Winter Vegetables

FREEZER/SUPERFOOD/PARENTS

Any root vegetable works good with this recipe. Try turnips, rutabagas, or beets for variety.

12 SERVINGS

1 large sweet potato

1 small butternut squash

2 medium parsnips

2 tablespoons extra-virgin olive oil

Salt and pepper to taste

1. Preheat oven to 425°F.

2. Peel all vegetables and cut into chunks. (Remove seeds from squash before cutting.)

3. Toss in olive oil, salt, and pepper, if using.

4. Spread in a single layer on a cookie sheet.

5. Bake until tender and sweet, approximately 20 minutes. Serve.

Summer Fruit Yogurt Coolers

FREEZER/SUPERFOOD/INSTANT/PARENTS

When the sun is beaming outside and you crave something refreshing, this should satisfy your taste buds and help cool baby off. Substitute whatever fruit you have on hand—be creative!

2 SERVINGS

2 strawberries

1 peach

½ banana

1 cup vanilla yogurt

1. Hull and clean the strawberries. Cut in half and place in the blender.

2. Wash and peel the peach. Remove the pit, cut into pieces, and place in the blender.

3. Peel the banana and remove any damaged spots. Cut into chunks and place in the blender.

4. Add the yogurt into the blender. Mix until a thin drink results.

5. Pour into popsicle molds and freeze for 24 hours until set.

Sweet Potato Biscuits

FREEZER/SUPERFOOD/PARENTS

These savory golden orange breads get a supernutritional boost in beta-carotene and vitamin C from sweet potatoes and applesauce.

16 SERVINGS

½ cup applesauce

2½ teaspoons baking powder, divided

1 cup Simply Sweet Potato (Chapter 4)

2 tablespoons extra-virgin olive oil

⅜ cup organic milk (dairy or soy)

3 cups white whole-wheat flour

1 teaspoon baking soda

½ teaspoon salt

1. Preheat oven to 425°F.
2. In a large bowl, combine applesauce with ½ teaspoon baking powder.
3. Add sweet potato, olive oil, and organic milk.
4. In a medium bowl, combine flour, 2 teaspoons baking powder, baking soda, and salt.
5. Slowly mix dry ingredients into wet.
6. Drop batter onto greased cookie sheet.
7. Bake 10 minutes.

Avocado Yogurt Dip

SUPERFOOD/INSTANT/PARENTS

Use this sweet and creamy dip as a salad dressing for yourself, or pull up a chair and serve this with pita or tortilla chips for a healthy snack.

1 CUP; 4 SERVINGS

½ ripe avocado

¼ cup plain yogurt

1 teaspoon agave nectar

2 tablespoons orange juice

1. Mash avocado.
2. Add remaining ingredients.
3. Stir until smooth.

Baked Pita Chips

PARENTS

These make great chips for snacking. Serve these with the Avocado Yogurt Dip (Chapter 7) or with the Chocolate Pomegranate Dip (Chapter 7).

48 CHIPS; 8 SERVINGS

6 whole-wheat pita pockets

½ cup extra-virgin olive oil

½ teaspoon garlic salt

1. Preheat oven to 400°F.
2. Lay out six whole-wheat pitas and brush both sides with extra-virgin olive oil.
3. Cut each whole-wheat pita pocket into 8 chips.
4. Sprinkle with garlic salt. Spread pita chips out on a baking sheet.
5. Bake for about 7 minutes or until pita turns brown and crispy.

Chocolate Pomegranate Dip

INSTANT/PARENTS

Commercial pomegranate juice is filled with antioxidants, offering three times more than both red wine and green tea. It's also an amazing source of potassium, which helps your kidneys, heart, and muscles work correctly.

3 CUPS; 12 SERVINGS

1 small package all-natural instant chocolate pudding

1½ cups organic whole milk

1 cup organic light sour cream

⅓ cup 100 percent pomegranate juice

½ teaspoon orange zest

1. Combine chocolate pudding and organic milk with a beater.
2. Once blended well, add remaining ingredients and blend until smooth.
3. Chill and serve.

Baked Tortilla Chips

PARENTS

Making your own tortilla chips is rewarding, especially if you can't find already made organic chips at the store. Serve these chips with the Pineapply Salsa (Chapter 7) or the Avocado Yogurt Dip (Chapter 7). Use whole-wheat tortillas instead of corn, or make them both and mix them up!

40 CHIPS; 5 SERVINGS

5 corn tortillas

Canola oil, for drizzling

Sprinkle of sea salt

1. Preheat oven to 350°F.
2. Cut tortillas into eight wedges each.
3. Drizzle a large cookie sheet with canola oil.
4. Spread tortilla wedges on the cookie sheet in a single layer.
5. Drizzle tops of tortilla wedges with oil and sprinkle with sea salt.
6. Bake 13–15 minutes until golden and crispy.

Grilled Summer Veggies

SUPERFOOD/PARENTS

Grill vegetables on the top rack of the grill if you have one for best results. Otherwise, place them in aluminum foil or in a grill pan so they won't burn or fall through the grate.

4 SERVINGS

1 head broccoli, trimmed into florets

1 yellow summer squash, sliced

3 fresh ripe tomatoes, cut into wedges

1 red onion, sliced

Extra-virgin olive oil, for rub

¼ teaspoon sea salt

1. Preheat grill.
2. Combine all ingredients in a large bowl, taking care to rub extra-virgin olive oil into vegetables.
3. Wrap vegetables in aluminum foil.
4. Place on top rack of hot grill for 5–7 minutes or until vegetables are tender.
5. Remove from heat and transfer to serving bowl.

Green Boats

Your toddler may be interested in trying these green boats once he knows they can set sail—in his mouth! This is a fun way to introduce celery. Get creative and see whose boat can sail around the plates and across the finish line into an awaiting mouth!

8–12 SERVINGS

4 washed celery stalks

1 8-ounce package organic vegetable cream cheese

Paprika seasoning

Organic Cheddar cheese slices, cut into triangles

1. Cut celery stalks into 4-inch pieces.
2. Spoon 2 tablespoons cream cheese into celery and level with a knife.
3. Sprinkle lightly with paprika.
4. Top each with a cheddar cheese "sail."
5. Cover, chill, and serve.

Lemon Raspberry Ice Pops

Instead of lemonade, try limeade, a twist on an American favorite.

3 SERVINGS

½ cup store-bought or homemade lemonade

¾ cup fresh raspberries

1. Combine lemonade and raspberries and purée.
2. Pour into a clean, empty ice cube tray.
3. Cover ice cube tray with aluminum foil or plastic wrap.
4. Poke a craft stick through a slit in each of the filled ice cube spots.
5. Freeze for 24 hours, or until solid, and remove foil or plastic wrap.
6. If it is difficult to get the pops out of the tray, run the bottom of the ice cube tray under warm water to loosen.

Roasted Potato Rounds

A quick way to coat the potatoes with oil is to combine them and the olive oil in a plastic bag and shake them all up! Add a splash of color by adding fresh parsley from your garden.

24 ROUNDS; 6 SERVINGS

3 large red-skinned potatoes
2 tablespoons extra-virgin olive oil
Sprinkling of sea salt
Dash of pepper

1. Preheat oven to 475°F.
2. Wash and thinly slice potatoes.
3. Spread 1 tablespoon extra-virgin olive oil on baking sheet.
4. Spread potato slices on top of oil.
5. Top with remaining oil and salt and pepper.
6. Bake 13–15 minutes, until soft and golden.

Orzo with Creamy Tomato Spinach Sauce

Spice things up by adding your favorite blends of seasonings or spices to the tomato sauce. Maybe there's even some fresh basil or rosemary ready for picking in your yard.

5 SERVINGS

¾ cup orzo (or other very small pasta)
½ cup plain tomato sauce
¼ cup silken tofu
¼ cup chopped fresh or frozen spinach, thawed

1. Cook orzo according to pasta directions. Drain and set aside.
2. In a food processor, combine pasta sauce, tofu, and spinach. Process until smooth.
3. Transfer sauce to a small saucepan. Heat through.
4. Stir orzo into sauce.

Strawberry Cantaloupe Sorbet

FREEZER/SUPERFOOD/INSTANT/PARENTS

Everyone in the family can enjoy this healthy dessert. Make sure the strawberries are sweet and flavorful or the sorbet may be a little tart.

8 SERVINGS (4 CUPS)

½ medium cantaloupe

1½ cups strawberries

½ cup 100 percent apple juice

1. In a food processor or blender, purée all ingredients together.
2. Pour into a freezer-safe container.
3. After 1½–2 hours, fluff sorbet with a fork; then return to freezer.
4. After 2 more hours, fluff sorbet with a fork and return to freezer.
5. Continue this process until ready to serve.

Sweet Potato Spread

SUPERFOOD/INSTANT/PARENTS

Serve this sweet spread to add a powerhouse of vitamins and antioxidants to muffins or whole-grain toast. This also pairs well with the Homemade Biter Biscuits (Chapter 7) or Baked Pita Chips (Chapter 7).

16 SERVINGS

1 cup grated raw sweet potato

¾ cup water

1 teaspoon maple syrup

¼ teaspoon cinnamon

⅛ teaspoon nutmeg

2 tablespoons cream cheese (dairy or soy)

1. Bring sweet potato and water to a boil, keep boiling for 5 minutes.
2. Reduce heat to low and stir in remaining ingredients.
3. Keep stirring until cream cheese is melted and all ingredients are combined.
4. Spread a tablespoon on whole-wheat toast or muffins.

Strawberry Applesauce

This is a popular flavored applesauce that many enjoy. Serve chilled for best results.

4 SERVINGS

1 Gala or Fiji apple
1 cup strawberries
¼ cup organic apple juice

1. Peel and dice apple.
2. Wash and cut strawberries.
3. In a medium saucepan, add all ingredients.
4. Cover and simmer for about 10–15 minutes, until fruit is tender.
5. Mash with potato masher or purée in blender to desired consistency.

Cinnamon French Toast Breakfast

Make a large batch of these on the weekend and freeze. These are great frozen and then reheated in a toaster oven for an easy weekday breakfast. Serve with real maple syrup. Top with fresh fruit such as bananas or blueberries.

8 SERVINGS

4 eggs
2 tablespoons whole organic milk
¼ teaspoon cinnamon
½ teaspoon vanilla extract
8 slices whole-wheat bread

1. Lightly oil a griddle and preheat to medium heat.
2. In a medium bowl, combine eggs, organic milk, cinnamon, and vanilla.
3. Dip each slice of bread in egg mixture and place on griddle.
4. Cook until golden brown on each side.

Peach Raspberry Compote

This compote pairs well with Cinnamon French Toast Breakfast (Chapter 7) or with Moist Yogurt Pancakes (Chapter 7).

4 SERVINGS

1 cup chopped peaches

1 cup raspberries

2 tablespoons apple juice concentrate

Simmer all ingredients until fruit starts to soften and break down, approximately 10 minutes.

Spinach Tomato Scramble

To add variety to this dish, serve it different ways in the coming weeks using dark leafy greens such as chopped collards or kale.

6 SERVINGS

3 whole omega-3 fortified eggs

6 organic omega-3 fortified egg whites

¼ cup whole organic milk (dairy or soy)

1 teaspoon extra-virgin olive oil

½ cup spinach, chopped in food processor very fine

½ cup tomatoes chopped or mild salsa

½ cup shredded Swiss cheese (optional)

1. Blend eggs, egg whites, and organic milk using a whisk.
2. Add 1 teaspoon olive oil to a medium skillet and heat on medium.
3. Once heated, pour egg mixture into pan and stir with spatula.
4. Mix in spinach and tomatoes or salsa.
5. Sprinkle with cheese, if desired.
6. Continue to stir and scramble until done.
7. Remove from heat and serve.

Banana Yogurt Milkshake

Use agave nectar or honey to sweeten this to taste. Also, different flavored yogurts add interesting and delicious variations to this treat. Add crushed ice for a thicker and cooler shake.

4 SERVINGS

1 banana

1 tablespoon lemon juice

8 ounces vanilla yogurt (dairy or soy)

1 cup organic milk (dairy or soy)

1 tablespoon ground flaxseed

Combine all ingredients in a blender. Serve.

Orange Pineapple Smoothie

For a thicker shake, substitute vanilla or plain yogurt for the milk. Use fresh banana instead of frozen, but add ice to make this smoothie cold.

4 SERVINGS

1 cup frozen pineapple chunks

½ frozen banana

¾ cup 100 percent orange juice

¾ cup organic milk (dairy or soy)

Blend all ingredients.

Cheesy Grits

This classic Southern dish adds a nice texture when combined with meat or vegetables. Try different variations including topping it off with bacon, shrimp, scallions, or broccoli. Tastes great any time of day, and everyone can enjoy.

4 SERVINGS

½ cup grits

2 cups water or chicken stock

1 teaspoon unsalted butter or trans-fat-free margarine

¼ cup Cheddar cheese (dairy or soy)

1. In a small saucepan, combine grits, water, and butter or trans-fat-free margarine.
2. Bring to a boil, stirring constantly.
3. Reduce heat, cover, and simmer for 5 minutes.
4. Add grated cheese. Stir until cheese is melted.

Spaghetti Squash with Italian Herbs

Serve this dish with pasta and marinara sauce for variety.

8–12 SERVINGS

1 spaghetti squash

2 tablespoons extra-virgin olive oil

1 garlic clove, minced

1 teaspoon dried basil

1 teaspoon dried oregano

¼ cup Parmesan cheese (optional)

1. Preheat oven to 350°F.
2. Pierce squash with a fork in several places.
3. Bake 1½ hours (1 hour for a small squash).
4. Cut in half and remove seeds.
5. Scrape flesh with the tines of a fork to form spaghetti-like threads.
6. Heat extra-virgin olive oil over medium heat.
7. Add minced garlic and herbs. Cook 2 minutes or until garlic is golden but not brown.
8. Toss "spaghetti" with oil and herbs. Top with Parmesan cheese if using.

Caribbean Baked Risotto

This creamy Italian rice dish cooks similar to long-grain rice. However, after the rice absorbs the broth or stock, a nice creamy sauce remains. Risotto is traditionally cooked on the stovetop, but baking it allows you to get something else done in the meantime.

9 SERVINGS

1 cup arborio rice

1 cup coconut milk

3 cups vegetable broth

½ cup canned pumpkin

1 cup pineapple pieces

½ cup cooked black beans

1 garlic clove, minced

1 cup spinach, chopped

1. Preheat oven to 325°F.
2. Rinse rice.
3. Combine all ingredients in a covered casserole.
4. Bake 1 hour.

Stuffed Pork Chop

Save time with preparation by purchasing a boneless pork chop instead of one with the bone in.

2 SERVINGS

1 pork chop

¼ cup applesauce

1 tablespoon soy sauce

1 small garlic clove, peeled

1. Preheat the oven to 350°F.
2. Using a sharp knife, slice the chop in half horizontally about three-fourths of the way through.
3. Stuff the applesauce into the cavity.
4. Place the pork in an ovenproof baking dish. Spoon the soy sauce and garlic over the top, and bake for 40–50 minutes, or until the pork reaches 165°F.
5. Remove the garlic and discard. Slice pork into small pieces before serving.

Baked Veggie Risotto Bowl

This dish delivers carbohydrates, superfoods, and protein in one meal. Serve it alone or with baked cod.

5 SERVINGS
....
1 cup arborio rice

½ cup green beans

3 cups vegetable broth

1 cup broccoli florets

1 small zucchini, chopped

1 garlic clove, minced

1 cup cooked Great Northern beans

1 teaspoon dried basil

1 teaspoon dried oregano

1. Preheat oven to 325°F.
2. Rinse rice.
3. Trim ends from green beans, and cut into 1-inch pieces.
4. Combine all ingredients in a covered casserole dish.
5. Bake 1 hour.

Gobble Gobble Casserole

For an added bonus, try topping off this casserole with cheese and Italian-style bread crumbs for an extra special meal. Leftover holiday turkey and the drippings makes this dish extra easy to prepare.

2 SERVINGS
....
¼ cup broccoli

¾ cup chicken or turkey stock

¼ cup rice

½ cup cooked turkey, chopped

½ tablespoon unsalted butter

1. Wash the broccoli, cut into florets, and purée briefly in the food processor. You could also chop it into very small pieces instead.
2. Put the stock and rice into a saucepan, and bring to a boil. Add the broccoli, reduce to a simmer, and cook for 30 minutes, or per the rice package directions.
3. When the rice is cooked, add the chopped turkey and unsalted butter. Stir to mix.
4. Either serve as is or fork-mash before serving.

Creamed Tuna on Toast

SUPERFOOD/PARENTS

Because of its mercury content, take care to serve tuna sparingly. Many children also enjoy tuna on crackers with a touch of sea salt. For added color, try adding diced celery or peas.

1 SERVING

1 tablespoon unsalted butter

1 tablespoon all-purpose flour

½ cup milk (regular or soy)

¼ cup chunk light tuna

1 piece whole-grain bread

1. Melt the unsalted butter in a small saucepan.

2. Add the flour, stirring constantly until dissolved. Add the milk and continue stirring until it forms a thick sauce.

3. Turn off the heat and add the tuna. Stir until mixed and creamy.

4. Serve on top of a piece of whole-grain toast.

Haddock in Orange Sauce

FREEZER/SUPERFOOD/PARENTS

Orange zest comes from the peel of an orange and can be obtained by using a kitchen tool called a zester. If you don't have a zester, use a fine grater and rub the orange against it to obtain shavings.

2 SERVINGS

1 boneless haddock fillet

¼ cup orange juice

½ teaspoon orange zest

1. Preheat the oven to 350°F.

2. Rinse the fish fillet and remove all bones. Place in a greased baking dish.

3. Mix the orange juice and orange zest in a small bowl. Pour over the fish and spread the zest with a fork, making sure the fish gets an even coating.

4. Bake at 350°F for 15–20 minutes. The fish is cooked when it's opaque and flakes easily with a fork.

5. Spoon the remaining sauce from the pan over the fish, and cut into bite-size pieces before serving.

Hearty Veggie Soup

Vegetable soup provides warmth and comfort for children under the weather. The great part about soup is that you can add whatever vegetables you have on hand without making extra trips to the store.

3 SERVINGS

½ **cup green beans**

1 tablespoon unsalted butter or margarine

½ small onion, diced

1 medium red potato, diced

1 medium carrot, diced

½ cup kidney beans, cooked

Dash of salt and pepper

4 cups chicken stock or water

1. Snap the ends off the green beans, and then cut into 1-inch segments.

2. Melt the unsalted butter in a large saucepan. Add the onion, and sauté until it becomes translucent.

3. Add potato, carrot, green beans, kidney beans, salt, pepper, and chicken stock. Bring to a boil, and simmer for at least 1 hour. Longer cooking will make the vegetables more tender and enhance the flavors, but 1 hour is the minimum cooking time.

4. If desired, fork-mash the vegetables before serving.

Vanilla Maple Rice Pudding

This pudding tastes wonderful when warmed with fresh raspberries on the side.

8 SERVINGS

1 cup arborio rice

4 cups organic milk (dairy or soy)

½ cup maple syrup

2 tablespoons vanilla

1. Preheat oven to 325°F.

2. Rinse rice.

3. In a small saucepan, bring organic milk, syrup, and vanilla to a boil.

4. Combine liquid and rice in a covered 2-quart casserole.

5. Bake 1 hour.

Pearl Tapioca Pudding

SUPERFOOD/PARENTS

Tapioca pearls are primarily used as thickening agents in soups, stews, or pies. They resemble tiny pearls or small pellets and are used with milk to make a thick pudding.

2 SERVINGS

1½ cups milk

¼ cup pearl tapioca

¼ cup sugar

1 egg

¼ teaspoon vanilla extract

1. Pour the milk into a small saucepan. Add the tapioca and bring almost to a boil.

2. Stir and reduce the heat to a simmer. Cook for 6–7 minutes, stirring in the sugar as the tapioca simmers.

3. Beat the egg in a small bowl. Pour into the tapioca pot, and return almost to a boil.

4. Stirring constantly, reduce the heat, and simmer for an additional 8–10 minutes, or until the tapioca thickens up. Remove from heat and stir in the vanilla. Cool.

Tasty Tofu Scramble

SUPERFOOD/PARENTS

For a time saver, use frozen spinach that's ready to go and doesn't need to be washed or trimmed.

5 SERVINGS

1 tablespoon extra-virgin olive oil

1 garlic clove, minced

½ cup minced yellow onion

1 cup chopped spinach

15 ounces extra-firm tofu

1 tablespoon light soy sauce

1. In a large skillet or sauté pan, heat extra-virgin olive oil over medium-high heat.

2. Sauté garlic and onion until soft, golden, and fragrant.

3. Add spinach and sauté until wilted.

4. Crumble tofu and add to skillet.

5. Add soy sauce.

6. Cook over medium-high heat until heated through, approximately 7 minutes.

Tropical Fruit Smoothie

It doesn't have to be hot outside to enjoy a refreshing fruit smoothie. Make smoothies for everyone when it's cold outside for an instant indoor vacation.

5 SERVINGS

½ cup frozen pineapple chunks

½ cup frozen mango chunks

½ cup frozen strawberries

1 cup organic milk (dairy or soy)

½ cup 100 percent papaya juice

Combine all ingredients in a blender. Blend all ingredients until smooth.

Black Bean Burritos

Make this recipe when the night gets busy. Serve with a side of Mexican Fiesta Rice (Chapter 7). Roll the rice into the burritos or serve it on the side. It's healthy either way!

6 SERVINGS

½ cup black beans, mashed

½ cup grated carrots

1 cup cooked and shredded chicken

¾ cup organic shredded Cheddar cheese

3 whole-wheat tortillas

Mild salsa for garnish

1. In medium saucepan over medium heat, heat black beans, carrots, shredded chicken, and cheese until heated through.

2. Top each tortilla with ¾ cup of this mixture.

3. Roll up tortillas and top with salsa. Serve.

Mexican Fiesta Rice

Skip the store-bought packages of container rice for complete control over your own. Just add salsa and cheese to brown rice. You probably have some left over from last night!

8–10 SERVINGS

2 cups brown rice

½ cup shredded Cheddar cheese
(dairy or soy)

1 cup mild salsa

1. Cook brown rice according to directions.

2. Remove from heat and mix in cheese to melt.

3. Once melted, mix in salsa. Stir well.

Whole-Grain English Muffins with Cinnamon Butter

Store this cinnamon butter in a glass airtight container in your refrigerator. Use it as a flavored butter for waffles, pancakes, breads, and muffins.

8 SERVINGS

½ cup unsalted butter or trans-fat-free
spread, softened

⅓ cup honey

¼ teaspoon cinnamon

4 whole-wheat English muffins,
split in half

1. Blend butter and honey together with a beater.

2. Once blended, add cinnamon and continue to blend.

3. Toast whole-wheat English muffins and spread cinnamon unsalted butter on muffins to serve.

Apple Pear Crisp

Serve up this dessert with vanilla ice cream or frozen yogurt, and your whole family will be asking for seconds.

8 SERVINGS

3 medium pears
3 large apples
¾ cup packed light brown sugar
1 teaspoon vanilla
½ cup white whole-wheat flour
¼ cup old-fashioned rolled oats
¼ cup unsalted butter or trans-fat-free margarine, melted
Canola oil spray

1. Preheat oven to 400°F.
2. Peel, core, and thinly slice pears and apples.
3. In a small bowl combine brown sugar, vanilla, flour, oats, and unsalted butter.
4. Spray a 2-quart casserole with canola oil.
5. Spread fruit in bottom of casserole.
6. Top with sugar mixture.
7. Bake for 40 minutes.

MENUS FOR TODDLERS

Active toddlers need six small meals per day. Offer your child a variety of foods even if he refuses. It's normal for toddlers to graze, but don't substitute milk or sugary drinks for meals. Limit milk to 16 ounces per day and keep fruit juice to a minimum of 4 ounces per day. Plenty of exercise or physical activity makes for a hungry belly! **EVERY DAY: Whole milk:** 16 ounces per day **Typical pattern:** 3 meals plus 1–3 snacks

MONDAY	TUESDAY	WEDNESDAY	THURSDAY
Blueberry Pancakes	Whole-Grain English Muffins with Cinnamon Butter	Moist Yogurt Pancakes	Sweet Potato Biscuits and Sweet-and-Sour Meatballs
Pumpkin Risotto	Baked Chicken Nuggets; Mika's Rainbow Corn Medley	Creamed Tuna on Toast; Squash and Corn Combo with side of steamed peas	Black Bean Burritos
Orzo with Creamy Tomato Spinach Sauce	Haddock in Orange Sauce; Broccoli a la Pasta	Cheese Quesadillas with Tomato and Avocado; Mexican Fiesta Rice	Sweet-and-Sour Meatballs; Baked Veggie Risotto Bowl
Snack: Green Boats	Snack: Banana Yogurt Milkshake	Snack: Strawberry Applesauce	Snack: Lemon Raspberry Ice Pops

FRIDAY	SATURDAY	SUNDAY	
Orange Pineapple Smoothie	Blueberry Mini Muffins	Raspberry Strawberry Muffins	
Tuna Fishcakes; Roasted Potato Rounds	Mini Pizza Faces	Hearty Veggie Soup with whole-wheat crackers	
Chicken with Apricots; Minted Peas	Broccoli with Meat and Rigatoni	Cheesy Grits; Roasted Winter Vegetables	
Snack: Banana Bread	Snack: Chocolate Pomegranate Dip with fresh berries	Snack: Fluffy Lemmon Pudding	

INDEX

Note: Page numbers in **bold** indicate recipe category lists.